# Leading With Fun

*Infusing Joy and Laughter into Every Day*

Copyright © 2023 by Trient Press

All rights reserved. No part of this publication may be reproduced, distributed, or transmitted in any form or by any means, including photocopying, recording, or other electronic or mechanical methods, without the prior written permission of the publisher, except in the case of brief quotations embodied in critical reviews and certain other noncommercial uses permitted by copyright law. For permission requests, write to the publisher, addressed "Attention: Permissions Coordinator," at the address below.

Criminal copyright infringement, including infringement without monetary gain, is investigated by the FBI and is punishable by up to five years in federal prison and a fine of $250,000.

Except for the original story material written by the author, all songs, song titles, and lyrics mentioned in the novel Leading With Fun: Infusing Joy and Laughter into Every Day are the exclusive property of the respective artists, songwriters, and copyright holder.

Trient Press
3375 S Rainbow Blvd
#81710, SMB 13135
Las Vegas, NV 89180

Ordering Information:
Quantity sales. Special discounts are available on quantity purchases by corporations, associations, and others. For details, contact the publisher at the address above.
Orders by U.S. trade bookstores and wholesalers. Please contact Trient Press: Tel: (775) 996-3844; or visit www.trientpress.com.
Printed in the United States of America

Publisher's Cataloging-in-Publication data
Sorrintino, Phil & Susan
A title of a book : Leading With Fun: Infusing Joy and Laughter into Every Day

ISBN
Hard Cover      979-8-88990-150-1
Paper Back      979-8-88990-151-8
Ebook           979-8-88990-152-5

# What Do We Do?

We have been asked that many times as The "Original" Humor Consultants. We design and deliver customized solutions and results to clients from almost every conceivable industry. As the name implies, we use humor as a vehicle to deliver important action steps. We also provide consulting services to aid individuals and organizations in dealing with issues of self-motivation, change, sales, stress management, developing a desired culture and improving communication. We have worked with thousands of clients and have been in front of over a million people teaching them this message.

Since the company began in 1981, our mission is to "Create Results through Enjoyable Solutions." Our vision is to "Assist in the Enjoyment of Everything." (We think everything is a good niche. If you are going to pick a niche, pick everything.) What we really teach is the challenge the power and if you want it to be, the fun of freewill.

As Growth, Profit, and Enjoyment Advisors that increase employee engagement, we create tailored solutions that promote better teamwork, help people deal will stress associated with organizational change, and we create business systems that better communicate objectives.

# Chapter 1

## Introduction

Introduction

Thank you for reading this far (Ha-Ha), but before you go any further, you've got to be sure this book is really for you. So, here's what this book is about: transforming your company into a magnet for prosperity. Usually, small business owners and future entrepreneurs dismiss "company culture" as something giant corporations can afford to pay attention to. The idea is that as a small business owner your focus should be on the bottom line.

We have been brought in to help Fortune 500 companies and large corporations fix their workplace culture, and most of our conoaching (part consulting and part coaching) has been about reminding these business giants of their roots. We, for the most part, resuscitated their initial culture by reminding them of the importance of fun and positivity. So what's your takeaway? Corporations of the future must start with the right culture today. Millionaires of the future must start with the right mindset today. When you read this book, we can create that mindset together.

Let's create our world where laughter isn't just a byproduct of success, but a potent catalyst for it. In the bustling realm of business, where deadlines loom and stress often reigns, we invite you to don the cape of a Humor Leader and embark on a journey that will revolutionize your approach to leadership. This book, Leading with Fun, penned by the "'Original" Humor Consultants, is your passport to a workplace where joy is the driving force, where success and creativity blossom in the fertile soil of laughter. Get ready to step into a dimension where humor isn't a frivolous addition, but an essential ingredient for building thriving teams, fostering innovation, and nurturing a culture that thrives under the banner of positivity. So, put on your laughter-powered jetpack, because you're about to discover the art of leadership that doesn't just steer the ship – it turns the journey into an

    unforgettable adventure.

Discovering the True Essence of Leadership: The Confluence of Humor, Business, and Personal Growth

1. The Perspective Lens: Humor as Your Business Compass

We often define success in terms of revenue, growth, and market share. But what if there was another metric equally powerful? Phil and Susan Sorentino, the "Original" Humor Consultants teach us that our sense of humor is not just a jovial quirk, but a profound lens that alters our perception of the world. It's our very attitude. Thus, as entrepreneurs and leaders, we need to ask: what perspective do we choose? Do we opt for a loving, encouraging, and forgiving viewpoint or its counterpart? Remember, it's not about the jest; it's about the journey and the attitude we adopt along the way.

2. The Humor-Infused Leader: Breaking Stereotypes, Building Empires

Many have the misconception that serious times call for serious measures. Yet, some of the most challenging business situations have been deftly handled with a dose of humor. Infusing humor into leadership doesn't diminish the gravity of decisions or responsibilities; instead, it offers a fresh perspective, creates a conducive environment for innovation, and fosters resilience. By adopting Phil and Susan

Sorentino's philosophy of humor as an attitude, leaders can cultivate a workspace that navigates storms with a smile.

3. Personal Growth Through Laughter: From Potential to Prosperity

We can't lead others until we lead ourselves. Personal development is the cornerstone of effective leadership. Through humor, we can confront our fears, embrace our imperfections, and evolve continuously. It's not just about laughing at the world, but also laughing with it, and sometimes, at ourselves. This lighthearted approach offers a clear path to growth, allowing us to perceive challenges as opportunities, setbacks as setups, and most importantly, to understand the power of perspective.

4. The Positive Profit: Harnessing the Power of a Positive Outlook

Choosing a humor-oriented attitude isn't merely a feel-good strategy; it's a proven business tool. A positive, humor-infused environment boosts creativity, encourages risk-taking, and fosters team spirit. When employees look forward to Mondays as much as Fridays, that's the magic of a positive culture. And where positivity thrives, profitability isn't far behind. The takeaway? Don't just count your profits; make your profits count, with an attitude that amplifies abundance.

5. The Call to Transform: Your Next Step in the Business Odyssey

You hold the compass—the power to choose the direction of your business and life. Will you allow the hurdles to determine your narrative, or will you take the humorous route, viewing them as mere stepping stones? The journey of entrepreneurship is dotted with challenges, but with the right perspective—your sense of humor as your guide—you can navigate with resilience, grace, and most importantly, a chuckle. The next chapter is yours to pen, and perhaps it's time to sprinkle it with a bit of humor.

Remember, the journey to success doesn't have to be a solemn march; it can be a joyful dance. Embrace Phil and Susan Sorentino's wisdom and choose an attitude that not only elevates your business but also your spirit. After all, when work feels like play, success is not a destination but a delightful journey. Dive into "Leading with Fun," and embark on a transformative voyage where laughter isn't just the soundtrack but the fuel propelling you forward. So, dear reader, are you ready to laugh your way to the top?

Your Invitation to a Revolution

We've embarked on a brief exploration into the harmonious dance of humor, business, and self-development. But this is only the beginning. The real journey starts when you close this book and open your heart and mind to the infinite possibilities humor can introduce to your leadership style and personal growth.

We have been gifted with the profound realization that our sense of humor is the mirror of our attitude. It's a choice – a powerful one – that can influence not only how we perceive the world around us but how we shape it.

Take a moment. Reflect on the challenges and the triumphs you've faced in your business journey. Consider those moments when things seemed bleak or insurmountable. Now, reimagine those moments, but this time, see them through the lens of humor. Notice the shift? That's the power of perspective.

As you proceed with the chapters ahead, you'll be equipped with actionable insights, transformative tools, and a renewed sense of purpose. You're not just learning to infuse humor into your leadership; you're learning to reshape the narrative of your professional journey.

So, as you turn the pages of "Leading With Fun," remember that you're not merely reading a book. You're accepting an invitation to lead a revolution, one chuckle at a time.

Let's make the business world not just about transactions, but interactions - ones that are light-hearted, meaningful, and revolutionary. Onward, dear reader, to a world where profits meet positivity, where challenges meet chuckles, and where every obstacle is but a setup for a humorous punchline.

Take a deep breath, wear that grin, and step forward. Your revolution awaits!

# Chapter 2

## How To Use Positive Reinforcement To Help Your Team Perform Better

When you have a small business, you don't have infinite resources, and therefore small mistakes can cost big money. While corporations can afford to lose millions and still make a profit, every penny counts when you have a small business. It is, therefore, crucial to keep an eye out for mistakes. The problem with this mindset is that since you're looking for problems, you find problems.

From talks we have given about the Reticular Activating System to exercises we have developed for businesses to neutralize negative-leaning bias of the human perception; we have always emphasized the importance of adding weight to positive perception. Even if your only employee right now is yourself, you need to pay attention because we're sometimes harder on ourselves than we are to our fellow human beings.

Look around you: anywhere there is any dialogue, there's negativity from the social media comments section to news discussions. Why is that? Because our ancestors survived by keeping an eye out for what's wrong. We often bring up how, in ancient times, if something were moving in the jungle, it meant it could be food, or we could be food. So humans developed a mechanism to see what doesn't fit the pattern.

That's why babies grab things that aren't supposed to be on the floor. That's why we remember what we did wrong more than what we did right. If we're already aware of what's wrong, why fuel that and tunnel vision on what isn't working out? Instead, our experience has taught us that positive reinforcement is a better motivator and educator.

Start looking for what is right. This takes patience because you have to let your team members stumble across the right thing. You can be grateful and thankful for them following your directions, but ultimately, you're not training them to be blind followers. So, you might wait a long time before one of your employees does something that indicates autonomous interest in your company's success.

That's when you should unload all your praises. Let them and others know what a great thing the employee has done. Now you're not rewarding them for just following your directions; you're rewarding them for caring about your company. And that's something you cannot legislate. It is simple, but it isn't easy; you have to hold your tongue, avoid negative criticism, and wait till the first opportunity arises to open the floodgates of compliments.

While the first time might come after a long wait, the second will follow shortly because now your team has started noticing what happens when they care. They're incentivized to care without any overt contracts. From here on, you must stay consistent with the cycle till its effects ripple out into the entire workplace.

Laughter Lines and Bottom Lines: The Symbiosis

In the labyrinth of entrepreneurship, it's easy to get caught up in the immediacy of problem-solving, forgetting the power of perspective. But remember, perspective is just another word for attitude, and attitude, intertwined with our sense of humor, can change the game.

### Harnessing Humor as a Leadership Tool

Leaders often think they need to be serious to be taken seriously. But what if leadership was less about gravitas and more about light-heartedness?

When a leader learns to infuse humor into their approach, not only do they create a more inviting and enjoyable work environment, but they also open the door for enhanced creativity and innovation. The relaxed, humor-filled atmosphere becomes a breeding ground for new ideas, as employees feel free to express themselves without fear of criticism.

### Self-Awareness: Laughing at Ourselves

Personal development begins with self-awareness, and what better way to foster that than through humor? When we can laugh at our mistakes, we not only relieve the pressure of perfection but also pave the way for growth. By acknowledging our missteps with a chuckle, we open ourselves to learning, adapting, and ultimately, succeeding. And for those high-classed entrepreneurs out there: self-deprecation, delivered with a dash of humor, can be incredibly endearing, making you more relatable to your team.

### Creating a Positive Feedback Loop

In a world bombarded with criticism, both online and offline, why not be the outlier? Instead of joining the cacophony of negative feedback, craft a culture that's driven by positive reinforcement. Positive feedback, sprinkled with genuine appreciation and a touch of humor, not only boosts morale but also enhances productivity. When team members are recognized and celebrated, they're more likely to take ownership, exhibit loyalty, and go the extra mile.

Transforming Challenges with a Chuckle

Every company faces its fair share of challenges. But instead of perceiving them as roadblocks, view them as humorous anecdotes in your business journey. When teams approach problems with a humor-infused attitude, they're more likely to find innovative solutions. After all, humor requires us to think outside the box, to see the world from different angles. It's a cognitive flexibility that's a boon for problem-solving.

Inculcating a Humor-Driven Growth Mindset

A growth mindset, rooted in the belief that abilities and intelligence can be developed, becomes even more potent when coupled with humor. Embracing challenges, persisting in the face of setbacks, and viewing effort as a path to mastery can all be accentuated when approached with a light-hearted demeanor.

A Joyful Conclusion

Leading with fun isn't just about cracking jokes or fostering a laid-back attitude. It's about reshaping business narratives, fueling personal development, and revolutionizing leadership dynamics. It's about creating spaces where teams are excited to contribute, where ideas flow freely, and where every setback is just another story waiting to be shared with a hearty laugh.

In this expedition of entrepreneurship, where the path is dotted with uncertainties, why not equip yourself with the most potent tool of all - humor? Remember, it's not just about reaching the pinnacle of success; it's about enjoying the climb, one laugh at a time. Embrace this attitude, lead with fun, and watch as your business story unfolds, not as a series of stern chapters but as a delightful, humor-filled adventure.

The Final Chuckle: Turning Words into Wit-fueled Actions

They say a laugh is universal. It transcends borders, cultures, and even business hierarchies. And in the intricate world of business, where stakes are high and pressures run higher, a genuine chuckle might just be the secret sauce to not just surviving, but truly thriving.

So, let's reframe. Instead of envisioning a boardroom filled with stern faces and sharp suits, imagine a vibrant space echoing with ideas, punctuated with laughter. Envision team huddles that feel less like routine meetings and more like brainstorming sessions with a side of stand-up comedy. That's the power of leading with fun. It transforms the mundane into magical, routine into remarkable, and every challenge into a chance to chuckle and charge ahead.

But it's not enough just to imagine. It's time to act. It's time to infuse every email, every meeting, and every business strategy with a touch of humor. To celebrate wins with laughter and navigate losses with a grin. It's time to lead, not with fear or formality, but with fun.

Your Humor-imbued Homework

Your call to action? Start small. The next time you find yourself in a tense situation, try cracking a light-hearted joke. The next time you're in a meeting, share a funny anecdote. Slowly, you'll see the walls come down, the energy shift, and the collective morale boost.

And as you do, remember this: humor is more than just a tool. It's a mindset, an attitude, and perhaps the most potent weapon in your entrepreneurial arsenal. So, arm yourself with it.

Let "Leading With Fun" be more than just a book title. Let it be your mantra, your mission, and the legacy you leave behind.

So, dear reader, are you ready to infuse your leadership journey with a hearty dose of humor? Remember, every chuckle counts. Let's get laughing and lead the way!

# Chapter 3

## A Positive Perspective Creates A Positive Experience

The postmodern era has accelerated the business landscape to an increasingly materialistic one. From certain points of observation, it seems rather fair to deduce things for what they are on a material level. The assembly line model relied on this as far back as the time of Henry Ford. However, things have changed, and in a different context, the material lens is quite outdated.

Since most consumption occurs on the brand side of the economy as opposed to the commodity side, the human factor matters much more now. Reducing your workforce to material units will spell disaster because companies that choose to invest in their people as human beings will outlast those who try to operate their workers like machines. It is common knowledge that corporations are ruthless with their profit-oriented decisions. Still, the largest players in any market spend millions of dollars every year to train and entertain their people. It is no coincidence.

We hear all the time, " We train people and they leave." We respond, "What if you don't train them and they stay?" "We're here to tell you that you do not need to spend a lot of money when you're starting out: simply acknowledging your team's humanness counts a lot. When you can cultivate a positive outlook, you'll be an inspiring leader as opposed to the "boss." Some people refer to their boss as double S.O.B. backwards. While comical movie bosses get away with treating their workers badly, real-world businesspeople tend to be successful by having a high retention rate for their team and the clients.

To emphasize only one thing: believe that your people are good people. It is as simple as that. If you can give your colleagues, clients, customers, and employees the benefit of the doubt, you can instantly turn your work environment into a positive one.

"But Phil, Susan, we will get swindled this way!" you may protest. But if you hire right, you do not need to worry about that. In other words, take the pressure of doubting your employees' intentions and put it on the hiring process. Hire cultural-fits and value-matches, so you don't have these worries in the day-to-day operations of your business.

Similarly, take the pressure of doubting your customers every day and place it on targeting, so you get the right people into your funnel. The ultimate takeaway is that you should hire and market with this concept in mind: that you can afford to operate under the assumption that your customers and team members are people you can trust.

#*Laughter as an Empathy Bridge*

In a world increasingly dominated by technology, it's easy for human connections to fall by the wayside. The best leaders, though, understand that genuine connections are the bedrock of any successful business. As it turns out, humor plays a pivotal role in this. Remember, our sense of humor is our attitude. It reflects our perspective and, in turn, the way we view the world and those in it.

When you crack a joke or share a light-hearted moment with your team, it's not just about the punchline or the laugh. It's about acknowledging a shared perspective, a mutual understanding, and, most importantly, it builds empathy. It's a bridge that narrows the gap between authority and camaraderie.

Your sense of humor, therefore, is more than just a means to entertain. It's a reflection of your attitude towards your team and your clients. A loving, encouraging, and forgiving humor creates an atmosphere where people feel valued and understood. It's a powerful tool in your leadership arsenal.

Harnessing Humor to Boost Morale and Productivity

The right attitude can work wonders in the workplace. When approached positively, humor has the potential to rejuvenate the atmosphere, boost morale, and increase productivity. Think about those instances when you've had a hearty laugh at work. Didn't it feel like a weight was lifted off your shoulders?

By injecting humor, you're offering your team a break from their routine – a chance to let off steam. But more than that, you're also telling them that it's okay to be human. To err, to enjoy, to laugh. The subsequent environment is not only more relaxed but is also more creative, supportive, and collaborative.

## Your Humor, Your Brand

In the world of business, branding is everything. It sets you apart from the competition and gives your clients something to remember you by. But have you ever considered the role humor plays in this? Your brand's sense of humor reflects its attitude – whether it's confident, down-to-earth, or sophisticated.

Craft your brand's humor consciously. While it's essential to stay authentic, it's equally important to be sensitive to different perspectives. A joke that one group finds funny might not sit well with another. By ensuring your brand's humor is inclusive and considerate, you're not only building a positive brand image but also expanding your reach.

## Act Now: Embrace Your Humorous Side

No need to become a stand-up comedian overnight. Start small. Share a funny anecdote in your next team meeting, use a light-hearted tone in your emails, or celebrate small wins with humor-filled team activities. The goal is to show your human side – to demonstrate that leadership doesn't always have to be stern or formal.

Remember, as a leader, you set the tone. By embracing and promoting a positive sense of humor, you're opening doors to better relationships, a more inclusive work environment, and, ultimately, a successful business.

Leading with fun is not just a catchy phrase; it's a formula for success. By understanding and harnessing the power of humor, you're not only improving your leadership skills but also paving the way for a happier, more productive workforce. After all, a team that laughs together, stays together.

Leading Through Adversity with Humor

Navigating the treacherous waters of business challenges is a test of every leader's mettle. Yet, in those trying times, one's attitude – as reflected through humor – can often be the anchor that keeps a ship steady. While it might sound counterintuitive to infuse humor during crisis, let's dive into the rationale behind this assertion.

1. The Healing Power of Humor

Every entrepreneur, at some point, faces setbacks, failures, or simply unforeseen challenges. It's easy to fall into the trap of negativity or pessimism. However, leveraging humor during these times can act as a soothing balm. A light-hearted joke or anecdote can momentarily distract from the problem, giving everyone a much-needed breather. This isn't about avoidance, but rather a tactical retreat, allowing the mind to regroup and approach the problem with renewed vigor.

1. Humor Breeds Resilience

A shared laugh amidst a challenging project or after a tough meeting can make a world of difference. It fosters a collective spirit, a reminder that everyone's in this together. Such moments build resilience, cultivating a culture where teams can bounce back from adversities stronger than before.

1. Strategic Problem-Solving through Playfulness

Often, our most challenging problems find solutions in the most unexpected places. By encouraging a playful and humorous environment, you're indirectly promoting out-of-the-box thinking. When the atmosphere isn't stifling or overtly serious, individuals feel free to express unconventional ideas, leading to innovative solutions.

1. Creating a Safe Space for Constructive Feedback

Feedback, especially the constructive kind, can be hard to swallow. However, when delivered with a touch of humor, its sting lessens. By employing humor, leaders can create a safe space where team members feel comfortable sharing and receiving feedback, fostering an environment of continuous improvement.

1. Keeping Perspective in the Grand Scheme of Things

As we've learned, humor is essentially one's attitude. And sometimes, a humorous take on challenges reminds everyone that in the grand scheme of things, most setbacks are just temporary blips. This perspective encourages a growth mindset, where challenges are seen as learning opportunities rather than insurmountable obstacles.

Championing humor, especially during trying times, doesn't diminish the seriousness of challenges faced. Instead, it provides a fresh lens through which these challenges can be viewed. It fosters unity, resilience, creativity, and open communication. As a leader, by adopting and promoting humor, you're not only setting a positive tone but also equipping your team with a powerful tool to navigate business adversities. Remember, it's not about ignoring problems but rather approaching them with the right attitude. After all, a leader who can laugh at challenges will inspire a team that faces them head-on with optimism and creativity.

*Forge Ahead with Humor in Your Heart*

As we draw this chapter to a close, let's embrace a profound truth: humor isn't merely a tool; it's a way of life, a lens through which we can view the world in all its myriad complexities. Our attitude, as reflected in our humor, can be a beacon, guiding us through the darkest nights and into the dawn of new opportunities.

Every entrepreneur, every leader, every individual on a journey of growth must recognize that while the road to success is fraught with challenges, it's our attitude that determines our altitude. By leading with fun, by fostering a culture of laughter, and by maintaining a positive perspective, we're not only paving the way for our own success but also creating an environment where every team member can reach their fullest potential.

The journey of business and personal development, like life itself, is unpredictable. But remember this: no matter how turbulent the seas, no matter how stormy the skies, a ship led by a captain with humor in their heart and a positive perspective in their mind is bound to find its way to the shores of success.

So, as you turn this page and venture forth into the world, hold humor close to your heart. Let it be your compass, your guiding star, your secret weapon. In a world that often takes itself too seriously, dare to be different. Laugh a little louder, smile a little brighter, and lead with an unwavering spirit of fun. Because in the end, it's not just about reaching our destination, but enjoying the journey along the way. Forge ahead with a chuckle, a grin, and a heart full of joy, for success is sweeter when savored with a hearty laugh.

# Chapter 4

# A Playful Attitude Reduces Stress

As a "solopreneur" or a small business owner, you may share the same concerns as some of our recent clients. Ever since we started helping small business owners set up their respective businesses for the same level of success as our Fortune 500 clients, we have seen the word "stress" more often than we have seen each other. And we're husband and wife!

Our advice to small business owners and future entrepreneurs is the same as our advice to supervisors with dozens of direct reports (people directly reporting to them): leverage a playful attitude to reduce stress. Even though stress is a natural response to taking responsibility, it isn't essential to your success. In fact, the easier time you have letting go of stressful thoughts, the longer you can stay in the game. We know a thing or two about longevity: we started out in 1981.

That is the year that President Ronald Reagan fired all the Air Traffic Controllers.

Start seeing your business as a game. You may be very competitive and want to win at all costs. Still, you do not need to have a horrible time. Get excited instead of being nervous. Start seeing obstacles as challenges. Above all, see your employees as your teammates. Just like your teammates in an online game can quit anytime, so can your employees. And while your gamer friend Jack may dip out of a game session mid-mission because his mom brought him a grilled cheese sandwich, your employees need to leave for more serious reasons.

Do you stop playing the game because one of your teammates left? No, you start another session because the goal is to have fun. Of course, you have more fun when you're winning, so you try to win, but you do not try to get your victory in a way that ruins the fun. That's precisely how business should be handled.

It is tougher to do because you have your money on the line, whereas with games, you only invest time. But time, too, is precious. You do not see gaming as "wasted time" and almost never compare it to your earning hours, to determine how much money you have lost by spending two hours on a game you didn't win. But when it comes to business, you may take every loss to heart and fixate on the money lost.

We believe that by having a playful attitude, you can treat every loss as a "paid lesson." We all need to unlock a certain number of paid lessons before we can reach our goals. But having a playful attitude allows you to have the journey you can look back on and smile. Create a fun environment by helping everyone at your office cultivate a similar attitude. Pass them this book so they too can be on the same page and see how your business productivity and engagement changes for the better, by leading with fun.

Injecting Humor Into Tough Conversations

We all have those days: tough board meetings, uncomfortable employee reviews, or tricky client negotiations. It's easy to brace ourselves for the worst, turning these scenarios into grim, stress-laden affairs. However, have you considered weaving in a touch of humor to lighten the atmosphere?

Remember, humor is an expression of our attitude – it's our sense of perspective. When the atmosphere in a room feels tense, a well-timed humorous comment can offer relief, breaking the ice and creating a more relaxed environment.

1. The Gentle Art of Diffusing Tension

Tense moments are like tightly coiled springs. Humor acts as a release valve, letting out some of that pent-up energy. When you can bring people to a place of shared laughter, you're tapping into a universal language that can bridge even the widest divides.

1. Fostering Open Communication

With the barriers down, people become more receptive and open. They're more willing to communicate and collaborate, which often leads to more constructive outcomes. When approached with humor, what might have been a confrontation can turn into a conversation.

1. A Reminder of Our Shared Humanity

At its core, humor reminds us of our shared human experience. In the face of disagreements or challenges, a moment of shared laughter can remind everyone involved that, at the end of the day, we're all human.

This sense of connection fosters empathy, making it easier to navigate tough conversations with understanding and kindness.

1. Cultivating a Resilient Culture

When leaders consistently use humor as a tool, it trickles down to the entire organization. Over time, this can lead to a company culture that views challenges not as insurmountable obstacles but as opportunities to learn and grow.

Empower Yourself: Be the Spark of Joy

As a leader, you have the power to set the tone. Instead of dreading tough conversations, view them as opportunities to showcase your positive attitude. It doesn't mean undermining the seriousness of the situation, but rather introducing a balanced perspective. A small, humorous comment or a light-hearted analogy can be all it takes to turn the tide.

Next time you're faced with a challenging conversation, take a deep breath, tap into your sense of humor, and remember that it's okay to bring a touch of lightness to the table. After all, when we lead with fun, we pave the way for solutions that are not only effective but also enjoyable.

Let's face it: The world of business is filled with highs and lows. But amidst the hustle, the challenges, and the relentless pursuit of success, there's always room for a good laugh. As you journey through the maze of entrepreneurship, remember that your attitude – expressed through humor – can be your most potent ally.

By choosing to lead with fun, you're not only crafting a joyful journey for yourself but also inspiring those around you to do the same. So, dear reader, as you turn this page and venture forth, carry with you the infectious spirit of humor. Let it be the wind beneath your wings, propelling you towards success with a heart full of laughter and a soul brimming with joy. After all, in the game of business and life, it's not just about reaching the destination but cherishing every playful twist and turn along the way.

Humor as a Leadership Tool: Unlocking Potential

The common misconception about humor is that it is just a mere distraction or a side activity, perhaps reserved for Friday evenings or team outings. But in the context of leadership, humor can be transformative. It is not merely a break from the ordinary but a tool to elevate the ordinary. If humor is an expression of our attitude, why shouldn't it be a guiding principle in how we lead?

1. Cultivating a Learning Environment

Mistakes are inevitable. In any organization, regardless of its size or nature, there will be moments of oversight, miscalculation, or just plain blunders. Often, the immediate aftermath is anxiety or fear of retribution. However, imagine a scenario where the leader, after ensuring there's no critical fallout, infuses humor into the situation. It not only diffuses tension but also turns the mistake into a learning moment. In such an environment, team members are less likely to hide their errors and more likely to be proactive in finding and implementing solutions.

1. Building Trust and Authenticity

Leaders who use humor and are not afraid to sometimes be the butt of the joke are seen as more relatable and authentic. This authenticity breeds trust. And in any organization, trust is the bedrock of collaborative and efficient operations.

1. Inspiring Creativity and Innovation

When the workplace is filled with humor, it breaks down barriers. Ideas flow more freely in a relaxed environment, and people are more likely to think outside the box. Humor encourages a culture where ideas are shared without the immediate fear of judgment, which often leads to innovative solutions.

1. Driving Engagement and Commitment

A workplace that values humor and fun is likely to have higher engagement levels. Employees feel valued, not just for their professional contributions but for their personalities and individualities. This sense of belonging fosters commitment and dedication, driving better results for the organization.

Practical Steps to Infuse Humor in Leadership

1. Start Small: You don't have to turn every meeting into a comedy show. Begin by sharing a light-hearted story or a fun fact. The goal is to set a relaxed tone.

2. Celebrate the Wins with Humor: Had a successful month? Celebrate with a humorous award ceremony or a fun activity. Not only

does it acknowledge the hard work, but it also reinforces the idea that hard work and fun can go hand in hand.

3. Encourage Team Members: Create spaces where team members can share their own humorous stories or jokes. Maybe a dedicated slack channel or a segment in your weekly catch-up.

4. Continuous Learning: Keep yourself updated with humorous content, be it books, shows, or workshops. It will not only help you in your personal development but will also give you fresh content to share.

Leadership is not just about strategy, numbers, and decision-making. It's about people, emotions, and connections. When humor becomes an integral part of leadership, it revolutionizes the way leaders connect, communicate, and create.

So, as you embark on the exhilarating journey of leadership, don't forget to pack your sense of humor. With every chuckle, giggle, and hearty laugh, you're not just creating a moment of joy but building a legacy of positivity, resilience, and success. Remember, it's the leaders who laugh, who truly lead. And those who lead with fun, inspire a world of endless possibilities.

Embrace the Power of Positivity

Imagine a world where every leader, every manager, every supervisor approached challenges with a hint of playfulness, a sprinkle of humor, and a heavy dose of positivity. The very fabric of the professional environment would transform. Offices would no longer be places of drudgery but sanctuaries of inspiration. Stressful situations would transform into platforms for growth and innovation. The weight of responsibilities would feel lighter, shared among teams bound together by laughter and mutual respect.

As you finish this chapter, reflect on the journey you've embarked on as a leader, whether you're a budding entrepreneur, a seasoned CEO, or somewhere in between. Understand that you hold in your hands the power to change, to inspire, and to lead with love, laughter, and limitless potential.

Don't simply chase success; redefine it. Success isn't just about numbers, profits, or milestones. It's about the journey, the lives you touch, the smiles you share, and the joy you spread. As you navigate the complexities of the business realm, remember to carry with you the simple joys of laughter, the power of a positive attitude, and the undying belief in the potential of human connection.

Close this chapter with a commitment to yourself: that you will lead with love, laugh in the face of adversity, and illuminate the path for others with your radiant sense of humor. Because in the end, it's not just about how much you achieve, but how joyfully you live every moment of the journey.

Let your legacy be one of joy, compassion, and relentless optimism. Embrace every challenge, every setback, and every victory with a playful heart and a cheerful spirit. And as you do, watch the world around you transform, one smile at a time. The road ahead is filled with endless possibilities – face it with humor, face it with fun, and lead the way to a brighter, more vibrant future.

# Chapter 4

# Using The Right Words — The Key To Communication

If you've had some experience working with large corporations, you would know that there's a lot of emphasis on language used in the workplace. People are given manuals and hours of training so they can use the right words with their customers and colleagues. Most new business owners miss out on the hidden benefits of using the right language. "I started my business to be my own boss, so I can say anything" is a sentiment younger entrepreneurs have. But if you want to build wealth and leave a lasting legacy, you cannot afford to bet your likability on words you may be tempted to say in the future. Right now, you do not know what words might appear in your consciousness two days from now. Why would you ever rely on something so unpredictable?

Of course, we don't mean that you have to control every word that comes out of your mouth. You should run your language through a subconscious checklist. It will be challenging to internalize; but if you want to be successful, you'll look forward to the challenge. Here are the three non-negotiable things your words should always try to do:

Clarify

Communication is nothing if it is not clear. If you're saying something, it is your responsibility to have the other party understand you. It is not theirs to understand you. By taking this responsibility, you take charge of your communication. Do not use words that can confuse your audience. Words don't give meaning; people give meaning to words. When I say dog, what kind of dog do you see? We see a white Bichon-Poo named Luigi.

Be precise

We love to encourage people to make a difference; that's why we do what we do. But soon, we realized we were bamboozled because even as professional communicators, we couldn't say words just to say them! Everything has to be packed as precisely as possible. If you take your audience's ear-time for granted, you'll lose them.

Engage

Speaking of losing listeners, you have to know that even with valuable information, if you bore your audience, you're out of business.

Engaging your audience involves being entertaining but also entails using words that do not discourage people. Negative words have the power to disengage people. Even words that supposedly have a positive message but include negatives can definitely disengage an audience. For instance, when people say they "can't wait" to watch a movie, they're positioning impatience as a compliment. Even if it is consciously accepted by others, it has a disengaging effect on a subconscious level. That's why we say we're "looking forward" to a movie.

Laughing at the Language of Business

Every business owner will eventually face a time when they are lost in a sea of industry jargon. While industry-specific language has its place, sometimes it becomes the very barrier that prevents clear communication. Ever attended a business seminar or workshop and left feeling you needed a dictionary? It's time to infuse some humor into the often stiff and complicated language of the corporate world.

Acronym Antics

Businesses love their TLAs (Three Letter Acronyms). While they can help streamline communications, they can also be a source of confusion. Imagine hosting a lighthearted session where teams come up with the most absurd interpretations for common industry acronyms. Not only is it a fun exercise, but it also reinforces the importance of clear communication.

Buzzword Bingo

Every industry has its buzzwords. From "synergy" to "disruption", these words often lose their impact due to overuse. Why not turn it into a game? Create a bingo card with the most overused business buzzwords. During long meetings or conferences, employees can mark off these words as they hear them. The first to complete a line wins. It's a humorous way to point out over-reliance on jargon and encourage clearer language.

The Literal Interpretation Game

Encourage teams to come up with literal interpretations of common business phrases. What would "thinking outside the box" look like if taken literally? How about "pushing the envelope"? This game not only serves as a fun break but also underscores the importance of avoiding clichés in communication.

## Harness the Power of Humorous Stories

Humans are hardwired for stories. Storytelling is one of the most effective ways to communicate, especially when the subject matter is complex or tedious. When combined with humor, stories become even more powerful.

### Share Personal Anecdotes

Share a funny incident or misunderstanding from your own journey in the business world. Not only does this make you more relatable, but it also makes the lesson more memorable. It could be about the time you misunderstood a business term, or when a cultural faux pas led to a hilarious situation during an overseas conference.

### The Misadventures of a Fictional Character

Create a fictional character who frequently finds themselves in humorous business situations. Perhaps it's "Bumbling Bob", the well-meaning but often confused entrepreneur. By weaving lessons into Bob's misadventures, you can convey important business principles in an engaging manner.

Leading with Humor: A Journey of Continuous Learning

As you embark on your path of leading with fun, remember that humor is a skill, just like any other. It requires practice, refinement, and sometimes, learning from missteps. Start by observing comedians, noting the structure of their jokes, their timing, and their delivery. Apply these observations to your own humorous endeavors. Attend workshops or classes focused on humor and comedic writing. These will equip you with tools to weave humor seamlessly into your business communications.

Above all, be authentic. Humor, as defined by our sense of perspective, reflects our unique worldview. It's deeply personal. While you can and should learn from others, always ensure that your humor is a genuine reflection of who you are.

Remember, in the vast sea of business communications, humor is your lighthouse. It draws people in, breaks barriers, and illuminates the path forward. As you harness the power of humor in your communications, you're not just conveying information. You're connecting, engaging, and building relationships, one laugh at a time. So, embrace the journey, cherish the chuckles, and lead with laughter. After all, when words fail, a smile speaks volumes.

## The Subtle Art of Light-Hearted Listening

While a lot of emphasis is put on speaking and expressing, the art of listening, particularly light-hearted listening, often goes unnoticed. Business magnates and successful entrepreneurs all know the power of being an effective listener. But what sets apart a "humor consultant" from others is the way we approach listening — with a sprinkle of humor and a dash of empathy.

### Playful Paraphrasing

When you actively listen to someone, try paraphrasing what they've said in a playful manner. This not only ensures you understood them correctly but also adds a touch of lightness to the conversation. For instance, if a colleague says, "I'm overwhelmed with this project," you can respond, "So, you're saying the project's been a bit like juggling flaming torches?"

### Finding the Silver Lining

When faced with challenges, humor can help identify the silver lining. If a team member expresses a problem, take a moment to find a humorous side to it. It might not solve the problem immediately, but it certainly lightens the mood and can pave the way for creative solutions.

## Redefining Professional Relationships with Humor

Professional relationships are often seen as strictly formal, bound by the confines of corporate decorum. However, infusing these relationships with humor can lead to more genuine connections, fostering a sense of camaraderie and mutual respect.

### Humorous Icebreakers

Whether it's a team-building exercise or an introduction to a new client, start with a light-hearted icebreaker. Perhaps a funny anecdote or a quirky fact. This immediately sets a tone of approachability and authenticity.

### Compliments with a Twist

Instead of the regular "good job" or "well done", throw in humorous compliments. "You're the Batman of data analysis!" or "If problem-solving was an art, you'd be Picasso!" Such compliments are not only memorable but also bring a smile to the recipient's face.

## Business Growth Through the Lens of Humor

Expanding your business and navigating the market's complexities can seem daunting. But viewing this journey with a sense of humor can be a game-changer. Business growth, after all, is filled with moments of unpredictability, much like a comedy movie with its surprising twists and turns.

Celebrating the 'Oops' Moments

Every entrepreneur will face setbacks. Instead of dwelling on them, celebrate these 'oops' moments. Host a monthly "Oops Awards" where team members can share their funny mistakes. It cultivates an environment where errors are seen as part of the learning curve, not as failures.

Client Relations with a Chuckle

Building and maintaining client relationships is crucial for business growth. Infuse your interactions with light-hearted humor. Maybe it's a funny card accompanying your product or a humorous update email. Clients will appreciate the personal touch, making your business stand out in their minds.

Elevate Personal Growth with Laughter

As entrepreneurs, personal growth and business growth go hand in hand. Embracing humor in personal development leads to a more resilient, adaptable, and positive entrepreneurial spirit.

Humorous Reflection

At the end of each week, reflect on your highs and lows, but with a humorous twist. Maybe you had a "Why did the chicken cross the road?" kind of day. Reflecting with humor offers a fresh perspective, making challenges seem less intimidating.

Setting 'Fun' Goals

While setting your business and personal growth goals, add a 'fun' goal. It could be mastering a new joke each week or watching a comedy show. This ensures you're continuously feeding your sense of humor, an essential tool in your entrepreneurial journey.

As you navigate the exhilarating world of business and entrepreneurship, let humor be your constant companion. Whether you're facing challenges, celebrating successes, or simply going about your daily tasks, let your sense of humor — your unique perspective — guide and uplift you. And remember, in the vast expanse of the business world, it's those who can laugh at themselves and with others who truly leave an indelible mark. Keep laughing, keep leading, and let every chuckle chart your course to unparalleled success.

## Daring to Dance with Humor in Decision Making

In the rigorous world of business and personal growth, decisions are abundant, and they pave the path to our success. The way we view these decisions – through the lens of trepidation or with a sprinkle of humor – determines the ease of our journey.

### Tickling Your Brain

Every time you're faced with a tough decision, allow yourself a brief moment to view it with humor. Ask yourself, "What would be the most outlandish solution to this?" By doing this, you're not just seeking the funny side, but you're also kickstarting your creative juices, which may lead to genuinely innovative solutions.

### The Laughter Test

When mulling over options, consider which one makes you chuckle or brings a light-hearted feeling. There's wisdom in joy and amusement. A choice that brings a genuine smile might just be the one aligned with your inner truth.

## Unlocking Success with Humor-Driven Resilience

Setbacks, challenges, and hurdles – they're an inevitable part of the entrepreneurial journey. But guess what? They don't stand a chance against a spirit buoyed by humor. Every challenge is merely an opportunity to flex your humor muscles, demonstrating resilience that astonishes and inspires.

The Comic Comeback

For every setback, think of a light-hearted comeback. Missed a target? "Well, looks like I aimed for the stars and hit the moon! Adjusting my telescope for the next shot!" This attitude not only uplifts you but also sets a positive tone for your team.

Turning Lessons into Laughs

Every mistake holds a lesson. Transform each lesson into a light-hearted anecdote. This approach ensures the lesson sticks without dwelling on negativity.

The Ultimate Call to Lead with Fun

It's time to revolutionize your journey. We're not asking you to change the core of who you are or to discard the earnestness with which you approach your goals. Instead, we're inviting you to add a new tool to your toolkit – the profound power of humor.

Your journey will still have its ups and downs but imagine sailing through it with laughter as your wind and a light-hearted perspective as your compass. The challenges won't decrease, but your ability to handle them with grace and wit will skyrocket.

Remember, in the midst of negotiations, projections, and calculations, there's always room for a chuckle. This isn't about not taking your role seriously; it's about infusing serious roles with delightful energy.

Humor, your personal sense of perspective, is your most potent ally. It's your attitude, your shield, your motivator. Unleash it. Let it permeate every business strategy, every self-growth plan. Let it redefine success for you – not by the milestones you achieve but by the laughter lines you accumulate along the way.

So, put on those humor-tinted glasses, take a whimsical look at your world, and take the leap. It's time to lead with fun, to create, to grow, and to inspire. Because when you blend business acumen with a hearty laugh, success isn't just achieved; it's enjoyed.

Go on, tickle the world with your brilliance and laughter. Embrace every chuckle, every light-hearted moment. And as you do, watch as the world leans in, eager to be part of your humor-filled success story.

Here's to leading with fun, to unparalleled success, and to a journey that's as joyous as the destination! Cheers to you, the entrepreneur who laughs loudest and leads brightest!

# Chapter 5

# Conquer With Creativity

What is business success if not the result of creative problem-solving monetized? There's a lot to unpack there, and we must start with creativity. Do not try to take the easiest, most obvious path to your destination because that's one everyone is going to try. It is our firm belief that we developed from decades of consulting experience that the divorce between creativity and commercial aspects of business leads to a false dichotomy.

You shouldn't ever confine creativity to a few people in your business: it should be encouraged at all levels. Empower your team members to come up with creative solutions for any given challenge. That doesn't mean everyone will have the same level of decision-making and execution access. Still, it serves no one to shoot down ideas before hearing them out.

A great way some middle-management figures empower their teams while simultaneously decreasing the workload is by asking their direct reports to bring problems to them with a few solutions. You can take this and implement it in your business as well. When your people bring you problems, they are incentivized to just figure out issues. If you empower them with the responsibility to bring solutions, they get creatively engaged with the challenge at hand.

More importantly, they might discover a solution that doesn't require your approval. As a result, your attention isn't taken up by easy-to-solve issues. And whenever problems come to your desk, there are multiple solutions you can opt from right away. If you pick one of the solutions proposed by your team, you make them feel good while solving the problem without having to brainstorm. Speaking of brainstorming, we encourage you to have regular brainstorming sessions with your team. Creativity and ego are pretty close, and you don't want to confuse one with the other. Your business thrives from good ideas, not necessarily your ideas. Your ideas can be good, but that doesn't mean they're the best ones for every situation.

Ultimately, your success as a leader comes from picking the best idea, not thinking up the best one. So take that pressure off yourself and let your team feel invested in your mission by taking their ideas into the decision-making process. You still retain the right to execute or dismiss an idea, but if you're not going with an idea, you should use the lessons from the "using the right words" chapter earlier.

Humor's Role in Unleashing Creativity

If creativity is the vehicle for business success, then humor is undoubtedly the fuel. It's one thing to say you value creativity, but it's another to cultivate an environment where creativity thrives. And let me tell you, nothing fosters a more vibrant creative environment than a dose of well-placed humor. Why so?

Breaking Down Barriers

The pressure of coming up with 'the next big idea' can be paralyzing. When people are too concerned about saying the 'right' thing, they often end up saying nothing at all. A touch of humor helps lighten the mood, making everyone feel at ease. It serves as a reminder that it's okay to be imperfect, it's okay to be human.

Connecting Ideas with Levity

Think of the wildest, most out-of-the-box ideas that have emerged in the world of business. Now, imagine presenting those ideas in a room full of stern faces. Humor serves as a bridge, linking audacious ideas with their practical applications. When an idea is presented with a chuckle, it opens the door for others to see the potential humor and brilliance in it.

Brain Teasers and Chuckles

Start your brainstorming sessions with a light-hearted brain teaser. It can be something silly like, "How can we market shoes to centipedes?" or "How would you design an underwater laptop?" These questions, though seemingly ridiculous, get the creative juices flowing and set the stage for thinking outside the box. Plus, they bring a smile to everyone's face, ensuring the session starts on a positive note.

Embracing Creative Failures with a Laugh

All ideas aren't golden. In fact, the path to that one breakthrough idea is often paved with a myriad of 'not-so-great' ones. It's essential to understand and accept this as part of the creative process. But instead of sweeping these ideas under the rug, why not celebrate them?

The 'Whacky Idea of the Month' Award

Introduce a monthly award for the most outlandish idea. The key here is not to mock but to celebrate the audacity to think differently.

This not only acknowledges efforts but also fosters a culture where people aren't afraid to voice their thoughts, no matter how offbeat they might seem.

Giggle-Worthy Reflections

End your week with a light-hearted reflection session. Discuss ideas that seemed promising but didn't pan out and laugh over the quirks and unexpected turns. Transforming potential moments of discouragement into occasions of laughter fosters resilience and an eagerness to dive back into the creative process.

Your Action-Packed Humor Toolbox

Empowering your team with humor tools can have a profound impact on creativity levels. Here's a quick toolkit to kickstart the humor-driven creative revolution:

The Joke Jar: A jar filled with light-hearted jokes to be read out during breaks or at the beginning of meetings to set a jovial tone.

Humor Board: A board where employees can pin funny sketches, comics, or quotes related to the business. It serves as a constant reminder not to take things too seriously and to embrace the fun side of work.

Creative Timeout: A 10-minute session where the team indulges in some fun activity – be it a quick game, a funny video, or just sharing a laugh. It's like a mini-recess that helps rejuvenate the mind.

Whimsical Playshops: Organize playshops where the team learns the basics of stand-up comedy, comedic writing, or even improv. It's not just about the laughs; it's about thinking on your feet, connecting disparate ideas, and presenting them engagingly.

In the world of high-stakes business and relentless competition, let humor be your secret weapon. Use it not just as a tool to break the ice but as a powerful catalyst for creativity and innovation. Dive deep into the world of ideas with a chuckle, a wink, and an open mind. Because when you lead with fun, the journey to success becomes an adventure filled with laughter, learning, and limitless possibilities. So, ready to let your creativity soar with a side of giggles?

The Humorous Anatomy of Idea Evolution

Great ideas often evolve in stages, not unlike the life cycle of a butterfly. And just like the butterfly's transformation, each stage of an idea's evolution can be infused with humor.

1. The 'Wacky Idea' Caterpillar: The initial thought that wiggles its way into the brain might seem insignificant or even a little 'out there'. It's the offbeat idea that causes a chuckle or a smirk. Just as caterpillars munch on leaves, let this idea feed on conversations, brainstorming sessions, and a touch of humor.

2. The 'Let's Mull Over It' Cocoon: After the initial chuckle, let the idea simmer. Encase it in the cocoon of your mind, allowing it to gestate. This is the time for playful contemplation, doodling on notepads, or engaging in comedic thought experiments.

3. The 'Aha! It Might Just Work' Chrysalis: It's the moment when the humor-infused idea begins to take a more concrete shape. The chuckles of disbelief turn into chuckles of realization. The playful musing morphs into a structured strategy, but the humor never fades.

4. The 'Brilliantly Executed' Butterfly: The idea, now full of life and backed by a strategy, takes flight. It's colorful, beautiful, and still retains traces of its humorous origins. It's a testament to how creativity and humor, working hand in hand, can birth something truly exceptional.

Lessons from Comedic Icons: Embrace the Unexpected

The world of comedy is filled with legends who thrived on unexpected twists, turns, and punchlines. In the realm of business creativity, we can take a leaf out of their book. Embracing the unexpected not only keeps your competitors on their toes but also keeps your team's creative spirits high.

Think of it as the comedic twist in your business narrative. It's the product feature no one saw coming, the marketing campaign that breaks the mold, or the customer service gesture that leaves a lasting impression.

However, here's a word of caution: while humor and surprise are great, ensure that they align with your brand's message and resonate with your audience.

Cultivating the 'Yes, and...' Culture

Borrowing a principle from the world of improv comedy, the 'Yes, and...' approach is about building on ideas rather than shutting them down. When someone presents a concept, no matter how unconventional, the response should be an affirmation followed by an addition.

This encourages a flow of ideas, reduces the fear of rejection, and fosters a positive, collaborative environment. More importantly, it's a fun way to brainstorm! It ensures that the conversation is always moving forward, always evolving, and always infused with a touch of humor.

Wrap-Up: Cultivating the Playful Mind

Creativity thrives in a playground, not in a pressure cooker. By integrating humor into your business environment, you're essentially setting up a playground for ideas. A place where the swing-set of innovation meets the slide of strategy, all under the bright sun of humor.

So the next time you're at the crossroads of a challenging business decision or staring at a blank brainstorming board, remember to sprinkle a bit of laughter, add a dash of playfulness, and let the magic of creativity unfold.

After all, in the words of the "Original" Humor Consultants, humor consultant (wink, wink), "When in doubt, chuckle it out!" So, as you march ahead in your entrepreneurial journey, keep that sense of perspective alive, let humor be your compass, and watch as creativity becomes your most loyal ally.

Leading with Laughter and Legacy

We've navigated the colorful maze of creativity, laughed at our eccentricities, embraced the unexpected, and fostered a culture that thrives on innovation. But what does it all lead to? A legacy. A legacy where business is not just about profit margins and bottom lines, but about the joy of the journey and the stories we leave behind.

Dance to the Rhythms of Resilience: Every business endeavor comes with its share of highs and lows. It's the laughter amidst challenges and the ability to find humor in adversity that distinguishes the ordinary from the extraordinary. Dance through the storms, and when the music gets tough, remember to add your own fun beats.

Building Bridges with Humor: Beyond strategy and innovation, humor is the glue that binds teams together, creating a camaraderie that's palpable. It's the bridge between hierarchies, the common language that transcends barriers. By fostering a workspace where laughter is the norm, you're not only enhancing productivity but also nurturing a family that stands together through thick and thin.

Inspire with Your Legacy: As a leader, your actions echo in eternity. When you lead with fun and creativity, you inspire generations to view business not as a monotonous endeavor, but as a vibrant canvas waiting to be painted with innovative ideas and infectious laughter.

A Call to Arms (or rather, to Giggles!): Embrace this moment, dear reader. Stand at the helm of your ship, not with a stern face, but with a playful grin. Challenge the status quo, break the mold, and remember that every great idea often starts with a chuckle, a wink, and a 'why not?'

As we wrap up this chapter, take a moment to reflect on the journey so far. It's not about where you're headed but how you get there. And if you can get there with a belly full of laughs, a team that's passionately creative, and a legacy that resonates with fun-filled memories, you've truly conquered the art of 'Leading With Fun.'

Here's to the leaders who don't just direct but inspire. To the pioneers who blend wit with wisdom. And to every entrepreneur who knows that the real ROI is the joy of the journey. Cheers to leading, laughing, and leaving a legacy that lights the way for others. Onward and upward, with a giggle in every step!

# Chapter 6

## Preach Change By Not Preaching

Telling others they need to change is nothing but glorified complaining. True lasting change is inspired, not complained into existence. Unfortunately, educators have relied so heavily on "asking for change" as a tool to produce change that we've grown up defaulting to complaining. Think about it: what do teachers do when a student isn't acting the way they want him or her to act? That's right! They complain to the parents.

What do parents do if a teacher isn't instructing their child properly? They complain to the administration. As kids, we absorb this "easy" copout and start using it in our lives. We complain about the food we dislike and the clothes that we no longer want to wear. And that's where the most detrimental thing happens: our parents listen to us. At that moment, we realize that not only is complaining easy, but it is also effective. However, the complaint works only because our parents love us more than we can imagine.

You cannot take that "lesson" into the real world because complaining (or preaching) won't inspire the same need to change things among people who aren't motivated by primal instincts to make things okay for us. If you do not take any other lesson from this book, just take this one: talking about the need for change is an inefficient tool at best and must be discarded.

With that said, you have only one thing you can do to inspire change: dramatize its benefits in real life. Whether you do so by rewarding someone in your team who is behaving properly or behaving properly yourself and highlighting its benefits, you can portray the change you want. By dramatizing, we don't mean faking; the term just refers to bringing an idea to life through actions.

Of course, this is challenging to pull off for very specific things: if you need Jimmy to come to work on time, you can ask him to come to work on time. But for more abstract concepts that cannot be enforced through contracts (like positive thinking), words do not hold as much power as witnessed results. We work with small business owners to create such moments of revelation for their teams, friends, and even family members. No matter what positive values you want to instill in those around you, there is a strategy you can employ to inspire the results you want.

The Final Act: Leading with Laughter and Legacy

We've navigated the colorful maze of creativity, laughed at our eccentricities, embraced the unexpected, and fostered a culture that thrives on innovation. But what does it all lead to? A legacy. A legacy where business is not just about profit margins and bottom lines, but about the joy of the journey and the stories we leave behind.

Dance to the Rhythms of Resilience: Every business endeavor comes with its share of highs and lows. It's the laughter amidst challenges and the ability to find humor in adversity that distinguishes the ordinary from the extraordinary. Dance through the storms, and when the music gets tough, remember to add your own fun beats.

Building Bridges with Humor: Beyond strategy and innovation, humor is the glue that binds teams together, creating a camaraderie that's palpable. It's the bridge between hierarchies, the common language that transcends barriers. By fostering a workspace where laughter is the norm, you're not only enhancing productivity but also nurturing a family that stands together through thick and thin.

Inspire with Your Legacy: As a leader, your actions echo in eternity. When you lead with fun and creativity, you inspire generations to view business not as a monotonous endeavor, but as a vibrant canvas waiting to be painted with innovative ideas and infectious laughter.

A Call to Arms (or rather, to Giggles!): Embrace this moment, dear reader. Stand at the helm of your ship, not with a stern face, but with a playful grin. Challenge the status quo, break the mold, and remember that every great idea often starts with a chuckle, a wink, and a 'why not?'

As we wrap up this chapter, take a moment to reflect on the journey so far. It's not about where you're headed but how you get there. And if you can get there with a belly full of laughs, a team that's passionately creative, and a legacy that resonates with fun-filled memories, you've truly conquered the art of 'Leading With Fun.'

Here's to the leaders who don't just direct but inspire. To the pioneers who blend wit with wisdom. And to every entrepreneur who knows that the real ROI is the joy of the journey. Cheers to leading, laughing, and leaving a legacy that lights the way for others. Onward and upward, with a giggle in every step!

*Subtle Humor: The Silent Change Catalyst*

When was the last time you were in a tense meeting, and someone cracked a harmless joke, lightening the mood instantaneously? That's the power of subtle humor—it's the quiet game-changer in high-pressure business environments. It acts as a silent but potent catalyst that accelerates change, even when not vocalized explicitly.

Stories Over Statements: Instead of overtly pushing for change, weave humorous narratives that showcase the benefits of change. For example, instead of lecturing on the importance of punctuality, recount that hilarious anecdote about how being five minutes early once saved you from an awkward encounter with a spilled coffee cup or a misdirected presentation slide. The lesson? Early birds not only catch the worm but also avoid embarrassing hiccups!

Doodle It Out: A picture is worth a thousand words, and a humorous doodle might just be worth a million! Next time you're trying to convey a change in strategy, why not sketch out a light-hearted comic strip or cartoon? It's a visual, engaging, and laugh-inducing method that ensures your message stays imprinted in the minds of your audience.

The "What If" Game: Engage your team in a game of humorous "what ifs." For example, "What if our office was on Mars?" or "What if our products were used by superheroes?" Such questions stimulate imagination, challenge assumptions, and often lead to exciting insights about changes you might never have considered.

Mirthful Mirrors: Reflecting Growth with Glee

Business is not just about rigid numbers and hard facts; it's also about the human spirit's growth and evolution. And nothing mirrors this growth better than humor.

Shared Inside Jokes: Every business has its fair share of ups and downs. But the inside jokes stemming from past challenges? They're golden! They remind us of the hurdles we've overcome, the lessons learned, and the camaraderie built in the process. Every time a past challenge becomes a current joke, it reflects growth, resilience, and the ability to view hurdles with a sense of perspective.

The Humor Progress Bar: Just as you'd track a project's progress, why not track your team's humor quotient? Create a 'Humor Progress Bar' in your workspace. Every time someone cracks a joke, shares a funny story, or lightens the mood, move the marker up. It acts as a constant reminder that while you're serious about business, you're also serious about having fun!

Jovial Journeys: Charting the Future with Fun

Let's be honest; the roadmap to success is long and winding. But who says you can't enjoy the ride?

Whimsical Work Goals: Alongside your quarterly targets, set a few whimsical work goals. It could be anything from "Initiate a spontaneous dance break" to "Host a meeting in rhyme!" The underlying message? While chasing targets, don't forget to have a blast.

The Laughter Legacy: Future-proofing your business is crucial. But while you're laying down strategies for the next decade, also envision the laughter legacy you wish to leave behind. How do you want your employees, partners, and clients to remember you? As someone who not only scaled business heights but also added a touch of joy to every business day.

Final Chuckle: When Change Is the Only Constant, Laugh On!

In this ever-evolving business landscape, change is inevitable. But instead of resisting it, embrace it with open arms and a hearty laugh.

Remember, it's not the strongest species that survive, nor the most intelligent, but those most responsive to change (and perhaps, those with a hearty sense of humor).

As you close this chapter and gear up for the next, take with you the spirit of joy, the resilience of laughter, and the belief that every challenge comes with a hidden punchline. Because in the grand theatre of business, humor is the show-stealer, ensuring that every act, scene, and dialogue brims with potential and positivity. So, don your comedic cap, lead with fun, and remember: in the symphony of success, let humor be your crescendo!

The Echo of Empathy: Humor's Healing Touch

In the high-speed world of business, we often overlook the emotional toll of relentless pressures and demands. It's easy to forget that behind every project, report, or proposal, there's a human with feelings, dreams, and struggles. What's the solution? Empathy. And nothing radiates empathy quite like humor, a universal language of connection.

From Chuckles to Connection: Remember the last time someone cracked a joke during a tense moment? Not only did it break the ice, but it also bridged a gap, creating a shared experience of humanity.

Through humor, we send a signal: "I see you, I understand you, and we're in this together."

Gentle Teases and Team Bonds: Teasing, when done in good spirit and with mutual respect, can be a delightful way of strengthening team bonds. It's like saying, "I know you well enough to jest, and I trust our connection to understand it's all in good fun."

The Power of Perspective: Humor's Broadening Lens

Our definition of humor stresses on the sense of perspective. Business, with its inherent challenges, often narrows our focus, and we may lose sight of the bigger picture. Humor, with its widening lens, ensures we maintain balance and perspective.

Beyond the Tunnel Vision: Business decisions, when made with a constricted view, often lack foresight. A humorous anecdote or a light jest can serve as a reminder to step back, broaden our viewpoint, and see beyond the immediate.

The Flip Side Fun: Every situation has multiple facets. Training our minds to look for the humorous side of things is not just entertaining but enlightening. It's an exercise in creative thinking, allowing us to approach problems from unconventional angles.

## Harnessing the Energy: Channeling Humor into Productivity

Laughter is a burst of energy. Harnessing this energy and channeling it constructively can significantly boost productivity and morale.

Laughter Breaks: Introduce 'laughter breaks' during long meetings. A quick two-minute segment where team members share a joke or a funny incident. It acts as a mental refresh, rejuvenating the mind and ensuring the remainder of the meeting is productive.

Humor-Infused Challenges: Inject humor into regular work tasks. For instance, hold a contest for the 'Most Amusing Sales Pitch' or the 'Funniest Customer Interaction'. These not only add zest to mundane tasks but also foster creativity and innovative thinking.

## Redefining Success: A Journey Driven by Joy

In the relentless pursuit of success, it's easy to lose sight of what truly matters – the joy of the journey. The final destination becomes all-consuming, overshadowing the experiences, learnings, and moments of levity along the way.

Measuring Milestones with Mirth: As we set benchmarks and targets, let's also set 'joy milestones'. Celebrate not just the big wins, but also the small moments of laughter and camaraderie. These seemingly insignificant moments collectively contribute to a fulfilling journey.

Conversations Over Conversions: While conversion rates and ROI are crucial, the conversations we have, laced with humor and understanding, hold immeasurable value. It's these conversations that shape the culture, ethos, and soul of an organization.

A Symphony of Smiles and Success

As this chapter draws to a close, visualize an organization where laughter resonates in the corridors, where challenges are met with chuckles, and where every individual feels valued, understood, and connected. It's not a utopian dream but a tangible reality, achievable with the magic of humor.

Lean into the power of laughter, embrace the perspective it offers, and let it guide your path. For, in the end, it's not just about leading a business, but about leading hearts, minds, and souls with the gentle touch of humor. To a brighter, lighter, and infinitely more joyous tomorrow!

# Chapter 7

# Self-motivation Is The Only Motivation

In the previous chapter, we talked about inspiring change. This chapter builds on that idea and undercuts the hype surrounding forced motivation. Many motivational speaking businesses revolve around the idea that if you hire a speaker to come into your place of work and talk to your team for an hour, your team will be motivated enough to become magically more productive.

As leading company-culture and productivity-raising service providers, we could pretend that that's all it takes. If anything, that would drum up more business for us as lazier companies that don't want to change anything would think we're an easy fix. But we didn't get into this business for superficial displays of change. We have stayed in this business because of the difference we get to make.

And if you're going to have your own business empire in the future, you should learn this right now: internal self-motivation is the only motivation. That means you should hire people who are internally self-motivated and build systems around them that ensure that this self-motivation is maximized across a long enough period. That's why you need to have a great mission statement and the right company culture.

If you're not willing to hire and fire over culture, you don't have a company culture. If you're not willing to incentivize performance, you're not going to get the benefits of self-interest-driven productivity. While conglomerates bring in consultants like us to help fix their culture, you can craft your own culture by simply sticking to the two principles.

Hire for the right function

Employees get disengaged and might need exponentially rising rewards to stay engaged in "work" that they see as "work." That's why you should hire people in roles they enjoy. The number of cosmetic makeovers you give any job function can only take you so far in making it "fun" if the person you hired for it hates the actual work.

Turn "work" into "play"

When you hire someone who loves to clean for cleaning and someone who loves to type for typing, your job as a leader is pretty easy. Still, you have the responsibility of making sure the environment is conducive to humor. Make sure that work is taken seriously, and your team takes themselves lightly. We authored a whole book about that!

Solution-oriented questions

Everything changed for us when we stumbled across a fundamental truth: the questions one asks lead to the answers one gets. It seems obvious on the surface, but it isn't. People assume that whatever they perceive is reality. However, what Artificial programming scientists discovered is that before the 90s that there's no perception without embodiment or mission. When they tried to design artificial intelligence, it couldn't "see" the world because it didn't have a point of reference.

You don't see a ladder; you see something to climb and then call it a ladder. Similarly, you don't see "food" without seeing something "to consume." In other words, if you didn't know what consumption or climbing meant, you wouldn't be able to see ladders and food. When you internalize what this means for your everyday life, you will never ask questions like "what is the problem?" and "what's wrong?"

Since so much of our experience is directly a result of the questions we ask, we asked the question that would let us know what kind of questions we should ask on a regular basis. Phil and Susan, both of us, pondered for days thinking about this meta-question. We finally had our epiphany when life bombarded us with a total of eighteen problems in a single day. That inspired the following conversation:

"You know what's better than 18 problems?"

"19 solutions."

We agreed that the abundance of solutions was better than an abundance of problems. And soon, we had our meta-question: "How can we have more solutions than we have problems?" Just like we mentioned earlier in the book, the questions you ask lead to the answers you get. We got the answer the same night. If you want to have more solutions than the problems you have, ask solution-seeking questions. You can always rephrase any given question to be more solution-seeking. And a culture of creativity (see chapter: conquer with creativity) goes hand in hand with solution-seeking questions. Here is a handy list of solution-oriented questions:

1. What factors do I control?
2. In what ways can I use the assets I have towards fixing this?
3. What do I have that my competitors don't?
4. What am I not seeing?

5. What should I continue to do and why?
6. What should I stop doing and why?
7. What should I start doing and why?

And here is the most powerful question of all:

How can I turn this situation around in such a way that I am better off for having the "problem" than I would have been had it not occurred in the first place?

Harnessing Humor: The Subtle Shift To Success

Elevating a business beyond the common landscape requires not just ingenuity but also a refreshing perspective. The "Original" Humor Consultants insights into humor allows us to dissect this with precision. Humor, in essence, is a mirror reflecting our attitude. Imagine if every challenge in your business journey became a moment for laughter and every adversity an opportunity for a shared chuckle. The weight of the challenge diminishes, and what remains is the gleaming light of possibility.

A Laughable Ladder to Leadership:

If you ever observe children play, you'll notice how they incorporate humor effortlessly into every action, turning simple games into endless bouts of laughter. The corporate ladder doesn't have to be stark and mundane; it can be a slide, a teeter-totter, or even a merry-go-round if you allow humor to permeate its essence. By leading with humor, you open doors for easier communication, smoother delegation, and a cohesive team spirit.

Empathy through Humor:

Empathy is often a silent thread that binds teams together. Using humor, empathy can be channeled in a way that people feel seen and valued. For instance, if an employee is facing a challenge, a simple jest or a light-hearted analogy can make them feel less isolated. Such moments capture the essence of leading with fun - a fusion of heart, humor, and harmony.

Chuckle-Driven Goals:

Instead of traditional team-building exercises, how about a "funny story session" where every member shares the most humorous incident in their career? Or maybe a "Laugh-Off" where employees team up to bring the funniest ideas to a brainstorming session. These activities, though seemingly trivial, can cultivate a deep sense of camaraderie and ignite an environment of perpetual creativity.

Fun-filled Feedback Mechanism:

Feedback sessions are often daunting for both parties. But what if feedback was interspersed with humor? A playful metaphor, a jest, or even a light-hearted analogy can make feedback easier to digest and act upon. It reframes criticism into constructive banter, setting the stage for improvement without denting morale.

Finding The 'Ha-Ha' in Hardships:

Every entrepreneur faces challenges. But what if, instead of seeing them as obstacles, we saw them as humorous riddles waiting to be solved? This attitude, derived from our definition of humor, can reshape the narrative of hardships into adventurous escapades. For instance, a delay in delivery can be visualized as a race against time with playful detours.

Innovate with Intuition and Introspection:

While many leaders look externally for inspiration, there's a powerhouse of insight within, often brought forth with humor. The next time you're in a quandary, pause, introspect, and ask: "What would make this situation laughably easy?" More often than not, the humorous perspective will be the most intuitive one.

The Jestful Journey of Self-Development:

Personal growth isn't linear. It's a mix of highs, lows, loops, and leaps. And just like a jester brings joy to a royal court, infusing this journey with humor can make it vibrant and vivacious. As you evolve as an entrepreneur, let every stumble be a dance move, every setback a comedic twist, and every challenge a humorous plot twist.

Mingle Mindset with Mirth:

The balance between a growth mindset and humor is delicate yet dynamic. Envision a scenario where each new skill learned is celebrated with a jest, and every milestone achieved triggers a shared chuckle. This not only amplifies the joy of learning but also makes the journey memorable.

A Rollicking Wrap-Up:

Embracing humor isn't about sidelining seriousness; it's about supplementing it with a touch of light-heartedness. It's like adding a pinch of salt to a dish, enhancing its essence without overshadowing it. By infusing your entrepreneurial expedition with laughter, you're ensuring a legacy that's not just successful but also spirited.

So, as this chapter draws to a close, ponder upon this: If life's a stage and we're merely players, why not make your business act a comedy rather than a tragedy? Lead with love, light, and lots of laughter, for in the orchestra of enterprise, humor is the tune that makes the heart flutter. Embrace it, elevate with it, and let every entrepreneurial echo be filled with fun and frolic!

Perspective: Your Powerhouse to Potential

The Business of Perspective:

Let's take a leap into the world of perspective. A business's success doesn't merely hinge on the services or products it offers. It thrives on the collective perspective of its leaders and employees. If humor, as defined by our understanding, is truly a reflection of our attitude, then it becomes the driving force behind this perspective.

Imagine a room filled with sharp-minded entrepreneurs. While most are drawn into the minute intricacies of the problems they face, one leader stands out. This leader addresses challenges with a light-hearted chuckle and a radiant attitude, representing the epitome of humor as a "sense of perspective". In doing so, they're not just finding solutions; they're transforming the essence of the problem itself.

Navigating Business with a Humorous Compass:

Every entrepreneurial journey sails through stormy waters. Instead of fretting about the impending waves, humor acts as a compass, guiding you to navigate these challenges. It's not about belittling the issue but shifting the lens through which you view it. It's seeing the silver lining, the comedic undertone, and the potential for growth and laughter even in adversity.

Creating Cultures of Levity and Legacy:

A business culture steeped in humor is bound to be resilient. The ripple effect of a light-hearted joke or an amusing anecdote can resonate deeper than pages of motivational speeches. It's about building an empire that not only excels in numbers but thrives in spirits, attitudes, and collective joy.

Personal Growth through the Prism of Playfulness:

Diving into the realm of personal development, imagine transforming every hurdle into a playful challenge. View every setback as a setup for a comedic comeback. The personal growth journey becomes less about grinding and more about gleefully navigating the maze of life.

Empathetic Elevation:

Empathy is often the bridge between leaders and their teams. By sprinkling it with humor, you not only understand but resonate with the emotions of others. It's the difference between saying "I understand your problem" and "Remember the time when I spilled coffee right before a major presentation? Let's tackle this with the same spirit!"

Engaging Endeavors with Enthusiasm and Elan:

Leaders often talk about passion, but it's the fusion of passion with humor that creates magic. Engage in projects with a twinkle in your eye, an infectious enthusiasm, and a jovial jest on your lips. This approach doesn't undermine the seriousness of the task but adds a layer of zest that makes the process enjoyable.

Evolving through Experiences and Exuberance:

As we climb the corporate ladder, let's turn it into a playful playground slide once in a while. Every experience, good or bad, becomes a story, a narrative filled with chuckles and learning. With humor as your partner, evolve not just as an entrepreneur but as a beacon of exuberance.

Delightful Decision Making:

Decision-making can often be daunting. But with humor as a tool, it's about viewing every choice as an exciting crossroad. "Should we expand to the west or the east? Well, considering the last time we followed the sunrise and found our biggest client, let's chase the sunset this time!" It's about making decisions with wit, wisdom, and a whimsical wink.

Let your entrepreneurial saga be a rhapsody, a delightful mix of rhythm, resilience, and revelry. As you pen down each chapter, ensure that humor graces every page, every strategy, and every venture. As leaders, let's not just aim to leave a mark but to imprint a legacy of laughter and luminosity. Remember, in the grand game of business, every move can be a masterstroke if played with perspective, passion, and of course, a pinch of playful humor.

# Chapter 8

## Positivity Demystified

We've previously touched upon the idea of leaning towards a positive outlook. In our book and course, Work Smart, Have Fun & Make Money: Being Strong During Challenging Times, we cover it in more detail. But why is it difficult to default to a positive view? Why are there more pessimists in the world than optimists, and why is the general consensus that realism isn't the same thing as optimism? The answer lies in the following acronym: RAS.

The Reticular Activating System is a cognitive circuit that seeks disturbances in patterns. It is said to have evolved due to disturbances being fatal to our ancestors. This is why we're subconsciously seeking things that don't fit our idea of how things should be. But the Reticular Activating System is not needed in a society where tigers aren't ready to pounce at you at any moment.

It doesn't make sense to have the same openness to negative emotion from pattern disruption as the people who died every time patterns were disrupted. If you do not receive paperwork at the same time as you usually do, you aren't going to have the same consequences as an ancient hunter who didn't spot his game at his regular time. Unfortunately, you can't talk your RAS into submission. You have to exercise asking positive questions to override it.

While RAS is quite powerful, it doesn't have complete control of your perception. We get to decide how much power we give it. That's why we control whether we're terrified of a horror movie or talk through it while laughing about how unbelievable it is. It is called "suspension of disbelief," but we think it is "access to belief." While horror movies have deliberate pattern disruptions to evoke uneasiness, we give our RAS access to our belief system so that we get to experience the movie as if it were real.

Similarly, when stressful situations occur, we're most likely giving RAS access to our belief so that it can play out a negative movie. You can simply choose not to let RAS do that. Once you know that RAS is oriented towards exaggerating the negative, you can simply choose not to let it play any scenarios in your head. Instead, you can use your conscious thinking and ask yourself positive questions.

While RAS is a primal system in our brain, so is our problem-solving system. You fight ancient biological circuits by employing other ancient biological circuits. When you ask a question that leads to a positive answer, you take your consciousness out of a negative pathway and put it in a system that results in positive thinking. It takes effort initially, but once it becomes an instinctive response, you'll naturally have positive thinking. Pass this chapter along to your team members so you can all be in the right headspace whenever a problem arises.

A great work-life

Executives often ask us how they can create a fun work environment to boost productivity, and that's not the right question. As a leader, your need to create a fun work-life must come from a place of empathy and not from a desire for profit. While profit is a priority in business, it cannot be at the cost of your people's wellbeing. Whenever profit is prioritized over your core team or your clients' wellbeing, the business cannot last.

Remember that your people spend a significant amount of their life at work. If you do not want them to have a dichotomy where they see only their life outside work as "their life," you need to start creating a fun work environment with the goal of creating a fun work environment. In other words, you should make fun work-life a goal in itself. And just like we mentioned in the book early on, the right questions will guide you to the right answers.

Of course, in our direct client calls, we can help optimize workplace fun to match a business's budget and give more case-by-case advice regarding the kind of activities that can be woven into the fabric of a company's culture. Still, that doesn't mean you cannot craft your own activities and set your own calendar. In fact, we encourage it and are including timeless principles to help create a fun work environment.

The Humorous Habitat: Creating an Environment that Amplifies Attitude

Understanding the profound definition of humor allows us to establish an environment where levity and positivity flourish. It's a matter of fine-tuning our perspective, using it as a tool, and creating a habitat where every challenge is met with a chuckle and every project undertaken with playful exuberance.

The Power of Perspective Playgrounds:

At the heart of any business lies its culture, and when that culture thrives on a perspective of playfulness, it's bound to leave a mark. Imagine a boardroom meeting where every challenge is visualized as a game. The goal isn't to win but to play, and in playing, discover innovative solutions. It's about viewing profit charts not as mere statistics but as thrilling roller coaster rides. It's the art of seeing a client pitch not as a pressured sales call but as an exciting storyline waiting to be narrated.

Empathetic Engagements & Enthusiastic Endeavors:

The bond between a leader and their team is fortified when both share a common language of humor. As leaders, we must delve deeper into understanding the aspirations, dreams, and even the playful side of our team. Organizing events where teams can showcase their humorous side or share an anecdote can foster a deep-rooted bond. Remember, when humor becomes the bridge, empathy becomes the destination.

Cherishing Challenges with a Chortle:

Let's reframe challenges. Every obstacle becomes a humorous riddle. Each delay, a dramatic pause before the punchline. It's about cultivating a mindset where problems are not barriers but playful banter waiting to be tackled.

Goal-setting with Gaiety:

While goals in businesses are often surrounded by pressure and timelines, let's twist the narrative. How about setting 'laughter landmarks'? Every achievement, no matter how small, becomes a cause for celebration and humor. Achieved a target? Celebrate with a team joke hour. Sealed a deal? Maybe initiate a playful meme contest.

The Continuous Cycle of Comedic Creation:

Creativity and humor go hand-in-hand. A relaxed, jovial environment is often the birthplace of the most groundbreaking ideas. By integrating humor into daily brainstorming sessions, not only do you make them enjoyable, but you also tap into the unadulterated creative potential of your team.

Leading with Laughter:

Taking the principles of this chapter to heart, a leader's role becomes pivotal. It's about setting the stage for a performance where humor is the star, and everyone plays their part with joy. As leaders, we need to be the torchbearers of this humor-infused perspective, demonstrating through actions that work can be effective, efficient, and equally enjoyable.

So, dear reader, as you turn this page, ponder on this: Why tread the serious, well-worn paths of business when you can dance along with a tune of humor and hilarity? Embrace the unique perspective of humor. Paint your business canvas with strokes of laughter, playfulness, and positivity. And remember, in the grand narrative of your entrepreneurial journey, let humor be the quill that writes the most delightful chapters. It's not just about leading with success, but leading with a smile, a spirit, and a sense of fun. Join us in this movement - make humor your business strategy and watch as the world revels in your radiant reverie!

The Ripple Effect of Radiant Humor

In our journey of exploring how humor, especially as defined by our unique perspective, can reshape business and personal development, we've treaded on the paths of positivity and the reshaping of challenges. However, humor isn't just an internal tool for personal growth or a leadership style. Its impacts ripple outward, affecting interpersonal relationships, team dynamics, customer relations, and even brand persona. Let's dive into these waters.

Laughter Lines of Communication

When humor becomes an intrinsic part of a business environment, lines of communication open effortlessly. Team members feel more comfortable expressing ideas, challenging norms, and offering solutions. Why? Because when humor is the backdrop, fear of rejection diminishes. Conversations become less about hierarchy and more about collaboration. After all, if we can share a laugh, surely we can share ideas too!

Client Conversations: Less Transactions, More Interactions

Imagine approaching your next client meeting with a dash of humor. Not only does this break the ice, but it also transforms the interaction from a strict transactional one to a more relational one. Clients appreciate the human touch, and what's more human than shared laughter? Infusing humor doesn't mean undermining professionalism. It simply means adding a touch of personality and warmth.

The Brand that Laughs Together...

In today's digital age, a brand isn't just about the product or service it offers. It's about the story it tells, the values it embodies, and the emotions it evokes. Brands that embrace humor in their messaging become memorable, relatable, and often go viral! They aren't afraid to show a playful side, to engage with their audience in lighthearted banter, and to make their mark in the vast world of online content.

Personal Development: Riding the Wave of Whimsy

Now, let's circle back to personal development. As entrepreneurs, the road to success is often winding, bumpy, and uphill. But here's a game-changer: how about surfing on this road with a board of humor? Every setback becomes a wave, every challenge a chance to show off a new trick, and every achievement a beach party!

Resilience Through Ripples of Laughter:

Embracing humor offers another profound benefit – resilience. When you laugh at problems, when you see the fun in failure and the comedy in crisis, you bounce back faster. Resilience isn't about avoiding falls; it's about enjoying the bounce back!

Laugh, Lead, and Let Go:

As entrepreneurs, we're often told to take charge, to be in control. But with humor by our side, we learn the beautiful art of letting go.

Not every situation requires our stress. Sometimes, it just needs our smile.

The Radiant Road Ahead

As you flip to the next chapter or even as you close this book, take a moment. Breathe in the essence of what humor, in its purest and most profound form, offers. It's more than just jokes and jests. It's a perspective, a prism through which the world appears brighter, challenges become opportunities, and life itself becomes a joyous journey.

So, why wait? Don the hat of a humor consultant in your own life. Let every business decision, every team meeting, every personal goal be sprinkled with the magic dust of humor. And as you tread ahead, remember: Leading with fun isn't just a strategy; it's a lifestyle. Embrace it wholeheartedly, and let the world bask in the glow of your laughter-lit path!

From Workspace to Funspace: Humor in Practical Application

Incorporating humor into your business isn't about making the next viral meme or cracking the perfect joke at a board meeting. It's about subtly integrating a humorous perspective into the very fabric of your company's culture. It's about transforming your workspace into a fun space. So, how do we make this transition? Let's break it down.

The 10-minute Morning Guffaw

Why not start the day on a lighthearted note? Instead of plunging directly into the demanding tasks, begin with a 10-minute session where team members share a funny story, a light anecdote, or even a favorite joke. This simple exercise can set a positive tone for the rest of the day.

Humor Workshops: A New Kind of Training

Entrepreneurs often invest in professional development programs for their teams. Why not include humor workshops in the mix? Designed to sharpen the wit and enhance one's sense of humor, these sessions can boost creativity, foster team bonding, and encourage out-of-the-box thinking.

Feedback with Fun: Lightening Constructive Criticism

Feedback is crucial for growth, but it doesn't have to be stern. By weaving in humor, constructive criticism becomes easier to deliver and accept. For example, instead of saying "The presentation was too long," one might say, "If that presentation were a movie, I'd need two intermissions!"

Client Engagements: A Memorable Touch

Remember those drab monthly reports? How about adding a touch of humor by including a 'Joke of the Month' or a fun fact related to the business? This not only makes interactions delightful but also ensures your business remains memorable in a sea of competitors.

Rewards and Recognitions: The Playful Way

Recognizing and rewarding efforts is a key part of any business. Amplify this by adding humorous titles like 'The Office Sunshine' for the person with the most infectious smile or 'Captain Coffee' for that team member always seen with a coffee mug.

Social Media: Let Your Brand Personality Shine

The digital realm is ripe for businesses to showcase their humorous side. Quirky tweets, playful campaigns, or even a light-hearted behind-the-scenes look at your company can engage audiences like never before.

Humor in Self Development: The Laughter Journal

Entrepreneurs, while guiding their teams, should also take some 'me-time'. Start a 'Laughter Journal'. At the end of each day, jot down one thing that made you chuckle. Over time, this simple activity can shift your perspective, making challenges seem surmountable and successes more joyful.

The Journey from Formal to Fun

As we've explored, humor isn't just an abstract concept but a practical tool to enhance business operations and personal development. It's about looking at the ordinary and finding the extraordinary. It's about turning mundane meetings into engaging brainstorming sessions, transforming tedious tasks into thrilling challenges, and viewing setbacks as setups for comebacks.

Dear reader, as we wrap up this chapter, a gentle nudge – infuse your entrepreneurial voyage with a dash of humor. The road to success, dotted with laughter, becomes not just an achievement to reach but a journey to cherish. In the world of business, where stakes are high and challenges aplenty, let your sense of humor be your compass, guiding you with lightness and leading with fun! And as you march forward, remember: the world doesn't just need more leaders; it needs more leaders who can laugh, love, and lead with luminous levity. Onward to a brighter, lighter, and more humorous tomorrow!

# Chapter 9

# A Great Work-Life

Executives often ask us how they can create a fun work environment to boost productivity, and that's not the right question. As a leader, your need to create a fun work-life must come from a place of empathy and not from a desire for profit. While profit is a priority in business, it cannot be at the cost of your people's wellbeing. Whenever profit is prioritized over your core team or your clients' wellbeing, the business cannot last.

Remember that your people spend a significant amount of their life at work. If you do not want them to have a dichotomy where they see only their life outside work as "their life," you need to start creating a fun work environment with the goal of creating a fun work environment. In other words, you should make fun work-life a goal in itself. And just like we mentioned in the book early on, the right questions will guide you to the right answers.

Of course, in our direct client calls, we can help optimize workplace fun to match a business's budget and give more case-by-case advice regarding the kind of activities that can be woven into the fabric of a company's culture. Still, that doesn't mean you cannot craft your own activities and set your own calendar. In fact, we encourage it and are including timeless principles to help create a fun work environment.

Gamify lead measures

Lead measures are things your employees can control. While they might not control how many potential customers say "yes," they do control how many leads they call. Turning such measures into contests can turn work life into a game.

Encourage competition as long as it doesn't come at the cost of cooperation

While you're encouraging competition, make sure you don't take it to the point where the company culture turns into "every man for himself." Create teams, shuffle members, and reward cooperation just as much as you reward competition.

Prioritize results of time spent being busy

When you start expecting every minute in the office to be spent doing "work," you incentivize your team to look busy. Instead, if you focus only on results and base the rewards structure on showing up and making the most of one's time, you'll have a more engaged workforce.

Employ seriousness only where necessary

Finally, make sure that your team is required to be "serious" only where it is crucial. For instance, if a client expects a serious attitude during a call, you can expect that from your team. However, there's no need to call Jimmy into your office because he smiles a lot and leans back while he is typing.

Congratulations on making it this far. One of the things that carry this book and makes it so readable is the emphasis on fun. Similarly, you too should make fun second nature in your life. Do not force it into your business. Shift your perspective so that fun is a priority in business and life. This philosophy doesn't just help business owners; it is great for future entrepreneurs as well. We provide consulting and coaching (conoaching) for individuals who want to have a more captivating presence in their personal and professional life. That's because we believe having fun isn't optional; it is essential.

We have established ourselves as conoaches in leadership, team retention, and business growth by developing a philosophy that is central to humor as your 7th sense. As the "Original" Humor Consultants, we have helped thousands of corporations improve productivity and build amazing work environments. With decades in business consulting, we have seen the economy transform into what it is now at the time of this writing: despite the fact that over 80% of small businesses have no employees, small businesses employ 61.7 million workers. That's 46.4% of all us. With this book, we aim to help small business owners as well as future entrepreneurs.

You have just discovered the tools that were previously harnessed by Fortune 500 companies to build inspiring work environments. You need to leverage the same tools so you can think big and build a company culture that invigorates your team. An internally motivated organization can overcome any challenge. And to be self-motivated and to stay self-motivated, take yourself lightly and your work seriously.

Personal Drive - The Comedy Behind Ambition

As the "Original" Humor Consultants with a knack for turning even the most serious situations into laughter-filled adventures, we've mastered the art of injecting humor into corporate wisdom. So, here's our take on why self-motivation is the superhero cape every individual needs and fun strategies to unleash your inner motivational powerhouse:

1. Personal Drive - Because Who Needs a GPS When You've Got Ambition

Self-motivation is like having your own internal GPS that guides you towards your goals. It's that little voice inside your head that says, "You got this!" even when your morning coffee didn't.

2. Ownership and Accountability - When You're the Boss of You

Picture this – you're the CEO of 'Me, Myself & I Incorporated.' When you're self-motivated, you don't need a boss to crack the whip. You're the boss and the whip-cracker, all rolled into one!

3. Resilience and Persistence - Bouncing Back with Brio

Ever seen a rubber chicken bounce back? Self-motivated folks are the rubber chickens of the workforce – they spring back from setbacks with a comedic flair that would make a clown jealous.

4. Continuous Growth - Life's an Improv Show, and You're the Star

Self-motivated individuals have this unquenchable thirst for knowledge and growth. They're like lifelong learners on a quest to level up in the game of life. Who needs power-ups when you've got self-motivation?

Now, onto the strategies that are practically as effective as a whoopee cushion at a board meeting:

1. Set Clear Goals - Aim High, Even if It's Just for the Office Donut! Define your goals like you're aiming for the last slice of pizza. Break them down into bite-sized pieces that you can chew on, and voila – you're achieving like a pizza-loving champ!
2. Find Purpose and Passion - Love Your Work Like You Love Your Wi-Fi! Unearth your passions and blend them into your daily tasks like adding sprinkles to ice cream. Suddenly, work is a whole lot sweeter.
3. Celebrate Small Wins - Because Finding Your Keys Deserves a Victory Dance! Dance like nobody's watching (or like

everyone's watching and they're thoroughly entertained). Celebrate even the tiniest victories because let's be real – surviving Mondays is a major achievement.

4. Surround Yourself with Positivity - Good Vibes Only, Please! Fill your bubble with uplifting pals and mentors who are like your personal laugh track. A positivity posse – you'll wonder how you survived without one.

5. Practice Self-Care - Treating Yourself, the Non-Caloric Way! Remember, self-care isn't just a bubble bath; it's indulging in hobbies, enjoying quality time with friends, or binge-watching cat videos. Because nothing says self-love like a good ol' cat-in-a-box video.

6. Stay Curious and Keep Learning - "You're Never Too Old to Color Outside the Lines!": Embrace your inner Sherlock Holmes and investigate the world around you. Learning isn't reserved for classrooms – YouTube tutorials count too!

7. Reflect and Adapt - "Life's a Sketch; You Can Always Edit the Lines! "Reflect on your ups, downs, and hilarious sideways moments. Adapt like a comedian adjusting their punchline. Mistakes are just plot twists in your comedy script.

Remember, while self-motivation is your trusty sidekick, a workplace with more laughter than a comedy club and a supportive team that cheers your every success can turn your career into the blockbuster hit you've always dreamed of. So, go ahead, embrace your inner humor hero, and let self-motivation be your comedic cape on this adventure called life!

## Harmonizing Humor with Hustle

Tying a delightful bow on the concept of personal drive, the key isn't about driving yourself to the brink but rather harmonizing your inner drive with the symphony of laughter. How, you ask? Well, let's delve into it.

The Laughing Ladder to Success:

While the journey towards success might seem like a climb, why not convert each step of that ladder into a comedic beat? With every ascent, find a reason to chuckle, ensuring that the journey is as delightful as the destination.

Empathy in Execution:

A nuanced understanding of our humor-centric definition showcases the intertwined relationship between humor and empathy.

As leaders and individuals striving for success, cultivating an empathetic outlook not only eases communication but also fosters an environment of mutual respect and understanding. When empathy meets humor, every interaction, every deal, and every task turns into a memorable anecdote.

Tickling Tough Times:

No journey is devoid of hardships. But armed with our humor-infused perspective, we can navigate through these trying times with an occasional chuckle. Faced with a hurdle? Laugh at its audacity and jump higher! Confronted with a setback? Chuckle at its timing and set forth with renewed vigor.

Call-to-Action: The Humor-Infused Hustle:

To all the dynamic entrepreneurs and go-getters reading this, it's time to revolutionize your work ethic. Don't just hustle; humor-infuse your hustle! Every morning, as you set your goals, sprinkle them with a dash of humor. When faced with a challenge, don't just brainstorm; have a laugh session. Convert your boardroom into a laugh room occasionally and watch as ideas flow with unmatched creativity.

Leading with Levity:

Now, to the esteemed leaders who are steering the ship, it's time to redefine leadership. True leadership isn't about being stern or commanding respect through authority. It's about leading with levity. Create an environment where every task is approached with enthusiasm, where every meeting is an opportunity to share a laugh, and where every success, no matter how small, is celebrated with a burst of laughter.

The Comedy Compass:

In the world of business, metrics, statistics, and data points often guide decisions. But let's introduce a new compass – the comedy compass. This isn't about making decisions based on jokes but rather adding a layer of humor to every decision-making process. Analyzing data? Look for the comedic patterns. Setting targets? Set a few humorous milestones. Drafting an email? Start with a light-hearted line.

Call-to-Action: The Light-hearted Leadership:

For all the business leaders striving for excellence, it's time to lead with a smile. Embrace the humor-centric perspective and weave it into your leadership style. Remember, a team that laughs together, excels together. So, let humor be the glue that binds your team, fueling camaraderie and driving performance.

In Conclusion:

As this chapter draws to a close, it's essential to reflect on the transformative power of humor. Be it personal ambition or organizational leadership; humor has the magical ability to redefine, rejuvenate, and revolutionize. So, let's pledge to make humor a daily habit, integrating it into our professional endeavors and personal aspirations. After all, in the grand theater of life, humor is the showstopper, ensuring that every act is met with applause and every exit is followed by an encore!

*#Unlocking the Ultimate Superpower: Your Humor-Infused Perspective*

There's a prevailing wind of change in the realm of business and personal development. It doesn't whisper; it roars with laughter, echoing the sentiments we've poured into this chapter. But as with any tool, humor's efficacy rests on the wielder's shoulder. It's your time to step into the spotlight and turn that chuckle into a transformative cascade.

Your Comedic Quest Awaits!

Every individual reading this book is on a quest. Whether it's scaling the heights of corporate success, steering a startup to uncharted territories, or finding personal growth avenues that resonate – the journey is deeply personal and profoundly impactful. And as with any profound journey, the travel companions matter. So, why not invite humor, empathy, and a light-hearted approach along for the ride?

Call-to-Action: Dive into Your Humor-Driven Odyssey

1. Laugh at the Unexpected: Every twist, every turn, every unforeseen challenge is a punchline waiting to be discovered. When faced with the unexpected, take a deep breath, find the humor in the situation, and laugh. It's not just a coping mechanism; it's an empowering one.
2. Share the Mirth: The most potent humor is the one shared. Be the beacon of light-heartedness in your workspace. Share a joke, narrate a funny incident, or just be the person who can find the silver – or should we say, humorous – lining in any cloud.
3. Embrace Your Humor Identity: Your humor is unique to you – a culmination of experiences, insights, and perspectives. Embrace it, celebrate it, and let it be the guiding force in your professional and personal endeavors.

4. Seek Out Humor: Sometimes, humor doesn't come knocking; you have to seek it out. Be it comedic podcasts, funny video clips, or just humorous anecdotes – make it a habit to seek out things that make you laugh daily.

5. Reflect, Laugh, Repeat: At the end of each day, week, or project, take a moment to reflect. Find the humorous highlights, the unexpected comedic turns, and the laugh-out-loud moments. Celebrate them, learn from them, and gear up for the next chapter of your humor-infused journey.

Embrace the Ripple Effect of Radiant Laughter

The beauty of humor, as defined through our unique lens, is its cascading effect. When you laugh, you're not just uplifting your spirits but also those around you. As leaders, entrepreneurs, and trailblazers, you have the power to set the tone for your team, organization, and even industry.

So, as we conclude this chapter, remember: Your journey, filled with ambition, drive, and goals, has a secret ingredient waiting to be harnessed. It's the power of humor – an attitude, a perspective, a superpower. It's not just about leading with fun; it's about leading with purpose, passion, and a chuckle that resonates.

Go forth, armed with this humor-infused arsenal, and paint the world with shades of laughter, joy, and light-hearted brilliance. Let's not just chase success; let's do it with a smile, a giggle, and roaring laughter echoing in our wake!

# Chapter 10

## Laughter Leadership: Navigating Success with a Comedic Compass

In today's fast-paced and often stressful world, humor has become an essential ingredient for success. Your mission is to help individuals and organizations harness the power of humor to create a positive and engaging environment. By leading with fun, we can transform interactions, boost morale, and foster creativity

In a world that moves faster than a caffeinated squirrel, humor has graduated from being a side dish to becoming the main course on the menu of success. We're not just about cracking jokes; we're here to sprinkle humor like confetti and help you turn even the most serious situations into laughter-packed adventures. So, fasten your seatbelts, because we're about to dive into the marvelous benefits of humor in different corners of life, especially for entrepreneurs and small business owners. Get ready for some rib-tickling enlightenment and a pinch of practical wisdom!

The Chuckle Chronicles: Benefits of the Humor of Life: Mind and Body Oasis - Stress Relief Spa: Humor's magical ability to trigger genuine laughter is like a mini-vacation for your brain. Stress? It packs its bags and leaves town when laughter moves in.

1. Social Glue and Relationship Gourmet: Ever seen two people bonding over a hilarious meme? Humor is like the secret sauce that bonds relationships. It transforms awkward encounters into delightful conversations, whether you're at a networking event or at a family dinner.
2. Communication Comedy Club: Humor breaks down communication barriers like a sledgehammer through a sandcastle. It turns complex ideas into easily digestible nuggets of wisdom, making your point stick like a catchy tune.
3. Team Spirit Circus: Picture your team as a circus troupe, juggling tasks and responsibilities. Now, add humor as the entertaining ringmaster - it brings everyone together, strengthens team bonds, and turns the daily grind into a joyful spectacle.

4. Innovation Wonderland: Remember Alice in Wonderland? Humor leads you down a rabbit hole of creativity. It encourages "outside the box" thinking, making innovation sprout like daisies in spring.

Tickle the Entrepreneurial Fancy: Practical Tips for a Humorous Business Odyssey:

1. Set the Playful Tone: Just like a good stand-up routine starts with a solid opener, infuse humor into your company's culture from the get-go. Whether it's quirky office decor or light-hearted email signatures, set the stage for a fun-filled journey.
2. Laugh All the Way to the Brand Bank: Your brand's personality can be as charming as a friendly neighborhood comedian. Inject humor into your brand voice, website copy, and social media posts. Who said business can't be amusing?
3. Embrace Quirks and Goofiness: Remember, even the wackiest superhero has his quirks. Encourage employees to embrace their unique personalities. An office dance-off or a silly hat day can make your workplace more colorful than a rainbow parade.

4. Lunch Break Comedy Central: Inject humor into team meetings and brainstorming sessions. Start with an icebreaker that gets everyone laughing and watch creativity flourish like a garden after a rainstorm.
5. Fail Forward with a Smile: Mistakes are the stepping stones to success, so why not trip over them with a smile? Share your comical blunders and the lessons learned. It's like a TED Talk, but with more chuckles.
6. Office Pranks (the Kind Ones!): Remember, a rubber chicken on a colleague's chair never hurt anyone. Playful office pranks create a lighthearted atmosphere and keep the giggles rolling.
7. Share the Laughter Loot: Reward creativity and humor in the workplace. Consider a "Jester of the Month" award for the funniest idea or the "Giggle Guru" prize for the best joke.

So, as you navigate the entrepreneurial rollercoaster, remember that humor isn't just a garnish on your success salad – it's the zesty dressing that makes every bite a burst of flavor. We are here to remind you that a hearty laugh is the rocket fuel for innovation, teamwork, and memorable business endeavors. So, go ahead, sprinkle humor like confetti, and let the world be your hilarious oyster!

Uplifting Performance with Playful Positive Reinforcement

We understand the importance of positive reinforcement in enhancing a team member's performance. Positive reinforcement is a powerful tool that can motivate individuals, boost morale, and create a supportive work environment. Here are some ways in which positive reinforcement can help your team.

We're thrilled to dive into the depths of positive reinforcement and unravel its wondrous effects on employee and team performance. Imagine positive reinforcement as a sprinkle of stardust – it makes people shine brighter, feel appreciated, and transforms the workplace into a constellation of success. Here are the magical ways in which positive reinforcement works its charm:

1. The Golden Unicorn Trophy: Instead of a regular Employee of the Month plaque, introduce a rotating "Golden Unicorn Trophy" that's as rare as its namesake. Award it to the employee who's shown exceptional dedication. Just imagine the laughter as your team tries to figure out where to put this mythical creature on their desk!
2. The "Dad Joke of the Week" Award: Encourage positivity by recognizing the team member who delivers the cheesiest,

groan-inducing dad joke of the week. The winner gets a homemade, laminated "Dad Joke King/Queen" certificate. The worse the joke, the better the prize!

3. The "Boss for a Day" Lottery: Create a lottery where one lucky employee gets to be the "Boss for a Day." They get to make all the decisions, including declaring a mandatory ice cream break or instituting a "Pajama Day" dress code. It's a hilarious way to keep motivation high.

4. Comedy Roast Appreciation: Have a "Comedy Roast" session to appreciate a team member's hard work. Lightly roast them with funny anecdotes and exaggerated tales of their achievements. Top it off with a "Roastee of the Month" sash they must wear proudly.

5. The "Dance-Off" Victory: Celebrate a big win or milestone by challenging your team to a dance-off. The winner gets a goofy dance trophy and the honor of choreographing the company's next flash mob routine.

6. The "Loud Applause" Button: Install a comically oversized "Loud Applause" button in the office. Whenever someone

accomplishes something remarkable, the whole office can hit the button, and it produces an absurdly loud round of applause.

7. The "You Nailed It" Socks: Gift an employee who's performed exceptionally well with a pair of socks featuring quirky designs like thumbs-up emojis, dancing chickens, or even their face. It's a fun way for them to literally "walk on sunshine."

8. The "Mystery Meeting" Prize: Announce a "Mystery Meeting" that's actually a surprise celebration. When employees attend, they're greeted with party hats, streamers, and a cake. It's a delightful twist on the usual corporate gatherings.

9. The "DIY Desk Makeover" Contest: Encourage positive behavior by holding a contest where the winner gets to "remodel" their coworker's desk with a theme of their choice. Think "Tropical Paradise" or "Outer Space Odyssey." It's like Extreme Home Makeover but for desks!

10. The "Punniest Email Subject" Award: Challenge your team to come up with the punniest email subject line each week. The winner receives a silly pun-themed trophy and, of course, bragging rights as the "Pun Master."

Incorporating these humorous forms of positive reinforcement not only boosts performance but also fosters a workplace culture that values laughter, camaraderie, and creativity. It turns the office into a place where fun and work happily coexist.

Because let's be honest, while laughter is encouraged, spraying your colleagues with seltzer might not be the best way to infuse fun into the workplace. We'll show you how to be the ringmaster of a workplace circus where joy and laughter are the main attractions. Get ready for a rollercoaster ride of hilarity that'll have your team laughing so hard they might mistake the boardroom for a comedy club (just don't tell HR).

*Attitude Anchored in Humor: Your Business's North Star*

When setting sail in the vast ocean of business, it's essential to have a navigational tool. For many, it's profit margins, KPIs, or traditional growth metrics. But for those who embrace a unique sense of leadership, the compass is humor. Remember the "Original" Humor Consultants' wise words that humor is essentially our attitude. It's that sense of perspective, the culmination of all the experiences and senses. Your attitude, tinted with humor, can indeed shape the way you lead, work, and grow.

Humor: The Elixir for Entrepreneurial Excellence

The Lighter Side of Decision-making: When faced with business decisions, especially the tough ones, approach them with a light-hearted attitude. It's not about making fun of challenges but ensuring that you're not weighed down by them. Remember, every business decision comes with its set of anecdotes, some humorous and some educational.

Empathy Elevators: Humor and empathy go hand in hand. By bringing humor into the workplace, you are inadvertently encouraging empathy. When you laugh at a joke or find humor in a situation, you connect with those around you on a deeper level. This creates a bond that's hard to break, fostering a culture of understanding and compassion.

Pioneering with Positivity: Entrepreneurs are, at their core, pioneers. They tread paths unknown, facing challenges head-on. But what if this journey was peppered with humor? Challenges wouldn't seem as daunting, failures would turn into learning curves, and innovation would become a joyful endeavor.

## Humor-led Self-Development for Entrepreneurs

Harnessing Humor for Resilience: Every entrepreneur will face setbacks. However, it's the ability to bounce back that sets successful ones apart. By adopting a humor-centric attitude, you're equipping yourself with resilience. You're learning to see the silver, and often humorous, lining in every situation.

Continuous Learning with a Chuckle: The world of business is ever evolving. As an entrepreneur, you're constantly learning. Why not add a dash of humor to this continuous learning? Attend workshops that incorporate humor, read books that offer insights with a side of laughter, and always be open to the humorous anecdotes that come with every learning opportunity.

Networking with Nuanced Humor: Building business relationships doesn't always have to be serious. Infuse your networking efforts with genuine, empathetic humor. Share a light-hearted story, laugh at a mutual business blunder, or simply approach networking with a joyful demeanor.

Embrace the Comedic Compass: Your Call-to-Action

Dear business trailblazers, it's time to recalibrate your compasses. Let humor be your North Star, guiding you through challenges, leading you to innovation, and ensuring that your entrepreneurial journey is one for the history (and humor) books.

Craft your business narrative not just as a story of growth and success, but as an anthology of chuckles, guffaws, and light-hearted moments. Let every chapter in your business book be filled with laughter, learning, and leadership. And as you turn each page, may you be reminded of the "Original" Humor Consultants words, emphasizing the power and choice we have in the humor we bring to our business world.

So, to all aspiring and established entrepreneurs, our call-to-action is simple: Lead with laughter, succeed with a smile, and let humor be the wind beneath your business wings.

## An Attitude of Altitude: Soaring with Humor in Business

Having traversed the vast landscapes of humor and its myriad applications in the business realm, it's evident that humor isn't merely a tool; it's a mindset. It's the altitude of our attitude, defining how high we soar in our entrepreneurial endeavors. Drawing inspiration from Phil and Susan Sorentino's perspective on humor, it's clear that humor isn't just about the punchlines. It's about the perspectives we choose, the resilience we forge, and the connections we foster.

The Final Act: Transforming Knowledge into Action

All this knowledge about humor's power is but a treasure trove waiting to be unlocked. However, treasures are most valuable when shared. Whether it's the "Golden Unicorn Trophy" or the infectious "Loud Applause" button, the essence lies not in the act but in the attitude behind it. Your playful approach to challenges, your light-hearted interaction with team members, and your embrace of positivity make all the difference.

Every chuckle in a team meeting, every shared meme on a group chat, and every silly hat day is a testament to the transformative power of humor. These aren't mere activities; they're symbols. Symbols of a culture that values joy, camaraderie, and a touch of the unexpected.

## Your Humorous Odyssey Awaits

Now, with the knowledge, insights, and a sprinkle of stardust, it's your turn to embark on this journey. Let laughter be your map, humor your compass, and joy the destination. For in the words of the legendary Charlie Chaplin, "A day without laughter is a day wasted."

Heed the Humorous Call: As you stand at the cusp of this comedic voyage, remember that embracing humor is not just about introducing fun activities; it's about adopting a new lens to view the world. A lens that magnifies joy, filters out negativity, and captures the essence of genuine human connections.

Light the Torch of Laughter: Ignite the flames of humor in your organization. Encourage a culture where laughter resonates in hallways, where ideas are shared with a chuckle, and where challenges are met with a grin.

The World Awaits Your Hilarious Take: So, pioneers of positivity, champions of chuckles, and mavens of mirth, step forth. The business realm awaits your unique touch. Illuminate every boardroom with your wit, charm every client with your joyful demeanor, and lead every venture with an unwavering sense of humor.

*Take the Leap, Lead with Laughter*

As this chapter closes, another chapter in your entrepreneurial story begins. A chapter shimmering with potential, waiting to be painted with hues of humor. So, dear reader, rise to the occasion. Channel your inner comedic genius, embrace the wisdom of the "Original" Humor Consultants, and infuse your business journey with laughter.

Remember, in the grand theater of business, while strategies, plans, and metrics have their place, it's the joyous laughter that echoes the loudest and lingers the longest. So, make the choice today: *Will your business narrative be just another tale, or a legendary saga of success sprinkled with laughter?* The stage is set, the spotlight's on you. Take a bow, crack a joke, and lead with fun!

# Chapter 11

## Building Rapport Through Laughter: From Awkward Handshakes to Hilarious High-Fives (Without Pulling Any Muscles)

Building rapport can be as tricky as trying to juggle flaming marshmallows – it's a skill, and it can get messy. But why stick with awkward handshakes when you can elevate your rapport game with high-fives that could rival a grand slam at Wimbledon? Build connections through laughter, where icebreakers are as smooth as a banana peel on a cartoon sidewalk. Get ready to build relationships that are stronger than a double-shot espresso and as hilarious as a stand-up comedy show.

Transforming Presentations with Humor: From Snoozeville Slides to Laugh-Inducing Slapstick (Without Actually Slapping Anyone)

Transforming presentations with humor is like turning a snooze-inducing PowerPoint into a laugh-out-loud comedy club. Sprinkle your slides with humor that lands better than a pie in the face (no actual pies involved, we promise). Your audience won't just be clapping; they'll be rolling with laughter, and you'll be the comedy star of the corporate stage.

Nurturing Creativity with Playfulness: Breaking Free from Office Shackles (Without Actually Hiring a Locksmith)

Creativity is like a mischievous pet that thrives in playful environments. It's time to break free from the office shackles and create a workplace that's more playful than a circus on a sugar high. Exchange the mundane for the extraordinary, where brainstorming sessions are as fun as a day at the amusement park. Say goodbye to creativity blocks and hello to ideas that flow like a chocolate fountain at a kids' party (but with less mess).

Spreading Joy in Workplace Culture: From Office Buzzkills to Office Clowns (Without Squirting Anyone with a Flower Lapel)

Office culture doesn't have to be a parade of office buzzkills; it's time to turn your workplace into a carnival of joy where everyone's the clown (metaphorically speaking, of course). Create a culture where water cooler conversations are filled with hearty laughter, and even the photocopier has a joke or two up its paper tray. Say goodbye to office politics and say hello to punchlines that keep your team in stitches. It's time for your workplace to become the comedy club everyone wants to join (just don't expect anyone to squirt water from their lapel).

With humor as your trusted sidekick, building rapport, transforming presentations, nurturing creativity, and spreading joy in workplace culture becomes not just a strategy but a barrel of laughs. So, get ready to lead with fun and turn your workplace into a hilariously productive haven of positivity!

Share Success Stories: Bragging Rights Without the Bragging (Okay, Maybe a Little Bragging)

Sharing success stories can be like telling your friends about the fantastic meal you had last night – it's not bragging; it's just sharing the joy (with a hint of bragging, let's be honest). Share success stories without making your team feel like they're trapped in an endless slideshow of your vacation photos. Get ready to sprinkle your stories with humor and make your victories feel like they belong on the comedy stage (minus the two-drink minimum).

Foster a Supportive Environment: Where "You Got This" Is the Official Office Motto (Unless "This" Is Taming Wild Elephants)

Fostering a supportive environment means creating a workplace where "You got this!" is the official catchphrase. Well, unless "this" involves taming wild elephants; in that case, maybe you should call for backup. Foster support and camaraderie with humor that's more reassuring than a fluffy pillow fort during a thunderstorm.

Encourage Autonomy and Ownership: Because Micromanaging Is So Last Century (Like Floppy Disks and Pogs)

Encouraging autonomy and ownership is like upgrading from floppy disks to cloud storage – it's the way of the future. Empower your team to take the reins without hovering like a helicopter parent. And of course, we'll do it all with humor that's lighter than a feather on a helium-filled balloon.

Recognize and Celebrate: Parties, Prizes, and Puns (Because Who Doesn't Love a Good Pun?)

Recognition and celebration shouldn't be as stiff as a corporate tie. Let's make it as fun as a party with prizes and puns that could make even the toughest critic giggle. From "Pun-tastic Employee of the Month" awards to celebrations that rival a New Year's Eve countdown, recognize and celebrate with a dash of humor that'll have your team smiling from ear to ear (pun intended).

Provide Resources and Support: More Than Just the Office Printer (It Also Makes Great Waffle Art)

Providing resources and support isn't just about the office printer and Wi-Fi passwords; it's about nurturing your team's growth like a gardener with a green thumb (and a sense of humor). Offer resources with a twist of playfulness that can turn even the most mundane equipment into a canvas for waffle art. Because who doesn't want a printer that moonlights as a waffle maker?

Foster Collaboration and Cross-Pollination: Like a Beehive Without the Sting (Or the Buzzkill)

Fostering collaboration and cross-pollination doesn't mean turning your office into a literal beehive (that might be a buzzkill). Encourage teamwork and idea-sharing with humor that's more inviting than a potluck lunch with endless dessert options.

Emphasize the Benefits: Because Who Doesn't Love "Benefits" (Especially When They're Not Dental Coverage)

Emphasizing the benefits shouldn't feel like reading the fine print on your dental coverage. Highlight the perks of your workplace with humor that's more enticing than free pizza on a Friday. Your team will be singing the praises of those benefits with smiles so wide they might need extra-wide doors to exit the office.

With humor as your trusty sidekick, you'll find that leading with fun not only makes the workplace more enjoyable but also more productive and successful. So get ready to transform your workplace into a laughter-filled hub of positivity and progress!

The Quest for Rainbows and Productivity

Picture this: you, the fearless leader, standing at the entrance of your workplace with a rainbow-colored cape billowing in the wind. You're not just a leader – you're a unicorn whisperer, decoding the secrets of positivity and spreading them like glitter on a parade float.

Unicorn Whispering 101: Decoding the Language of Rainbows

Unicorns might not have a dictionary, but they sure do have a language – the language of rainbows and sparkles. Positive leadership is all about understanding the subtle nuances of this mystical dialect. From the encouraging wink to the motivational nudge, communicate with your team in ways that would make even the most eloquent unicorn jealous.

The Magical Transformation: From Gloom to Glitter

Remember when your office felt as lively as a library during a power outage? Well, positive leadership is the spell that turns that gloom into glitter. With your wand of enthusiasm and cape of charisma, you will transform mundane tasks into dazzling adventures, and your team will follow you like a trail of stardust.

The Joyful Orchestra: Leading with a Laugh and a Song

Positive leadership is like conducting an orchestra where laughter is the melody and motivation is the rhythm. Orchestrate moments of joy, turning your team into a harmonious ensemble that performs with gusto, whether it's singing together during meetings or tapping out beats on imaginary drums during brainstorming sessions.

The Superpower of Smiles: Turning Frowns into High-Fives

Imagine smiles as your team's superpower – their very own cape of invincibility. Positive leadership equips you with the magic wand of humor, capable of turning frowns into high-fives and sighs into belly laughs. Be the superhero who rescues productivity from the clutches of boredom, one punchline at a time.

### The Quest for the Golden Ratio: Balance and Positivity

Just like finding the pot of gold at the end of the rainbow, positive leadership is about striking the golden ratio between work and play. Sprinkle the workplace with just the right amount of fun – not so much that it's a circus, but enough to keep everyone engaged and motivated, like a magician who knows the perfect card trick to dazzle the audience.

### Unicorn Wrangling: Nurturing a Unicorn-Infused Culture

Positive leadership isn't just about being a unicorn whisperer – it's about creating a unicorn-infused culture where positivity is as natural as breathing and laughter is the soundtrack of success. Cultivate an environment where unicorns roam freely, spreading joy, and making the workplace a fantastical haven of creativity and achievement.

### Leading with Laughter, Rainbows, and a Dash of Sparkle

Imagine yourself donning your rainbow-colored cape and riding off into the sunset on the back of a unicorn, leaving a trail of laughter and positivity behind you. With the power of positive leadership, you're not just leading a team – you're guiding them through a magical journey where every challenge is a chance to shine, and every day is a page in the storybook of success.

Remember, positive leadership is your ticket to becoming the unicorn-whispering, laughter-generating leader your team deserves. So, go ahead, channel your inner unicorn tamer and sprinkle positivity like confetti on the path to greatness! With a dash of humor, even unicorn whispering becomes a laughter-filled adventure!

From Yawns to Yippees – Unleashing the Joy

Picture your office as a land of yawning chasms and raised eyebrows. Now, imagine you're the joy-bringer, armed with a confetti cannon and a dance-off challenge. Transform your workplace from a monochrome Monday to a perpetual party where even spreadsheets wear party hats.

The Dance-Off Revolution: Office Edition

Tired of board meetings that could double as lullabies? Say hello to the dance-off revolution! Turn your conference room into a dance floor, where PowerPoint presentations are accompanied by funky beats and chart discussions involve synchronized chair spins. It's like a flash mob without the mob – just a room full of employees grooving to the rhythm of productivity.

Incorporate Fun, Not Chaos: The Art of Controlled Whimsy

Embracing a joyful culture doesn't mean turning your office into a bouncy castle (although that might be fun). It's about finding the delicate balance between work and play, like serving gourmet cupcakes on a trampoline – delicious and exciting without causing frosting disasters. Sprinkle controlled whimsy like a seasoned pastry chef making your workplace delightful without compromising on professionalism.

Celebrate Quirks and Oddities: Where Superheroes Wear Capes of Creativity

In a joyful workplace, quirks aren't just tolerated – they're celebrated. Imagine your team as a league of superheroes, each with their own unique power. From the Spreadsheet Sorcerer to the Coffee Connoisseur, every team member gets their moment in the spotlight. Create a culture where creativity is as common as paper clips and capes are as standard as business casual.

Engage in Creative Combat: The Battle of the Brainstorms

Brainstorming sessions can be as exciting as watching paint dry. But fear not, because we're introducing a new kind of combat – the Battle of the Brainstorms. Armed with Nerf guns and water balloons, your team can engage in creative warfare, generating ideas that explode like glitter bombs. This isn't your average brainstorm – it's brainstorming on steroids with a touch of silliness.

Fun Rituals and Office Shenanigans: More Than Just Casual Fridays

Casual Fridays are so last decade. Get ready for a parade of fun rituals and office shenanigans that make every day feel like a celebration. From Silly Hat Mondays to Office Karaoke Wednesdays, transform the mundane into the marvelous and turn your office into a laughter-filled playground.

Celebrate Wins with Flair: From High-Fives to Victory Parades

Victory doesn't just deserve a nod – it deserves a parade, complete with confetti cannons and triumphant music. Celebrate wins, both big and small, with the flair of a carnival ringmaster. Whether it's hitting targets or conquering challenges, your team will march through the halls like conquering heroes, powered by positivity and a few well-placed high-fives.

Where Cubicles Become Carnival Rides and Meetings: Turn into Mime Performances

Imagine your office as a wild carnival where cubicles are roller coasters and meetings are mime performances. With the tools of joyful culture in your belt, you're not just creating a workplace – you're crafting an experience, where every day is a parade, every challenge is a game, and every success is a standing ovation.

Remember, cultivating a joyful workplace culture isn't just about productivity – it's about creating an environment where laughter, creativity, and camaraderie flourish. So, grab your confetti cannon, put on your dancing shoes, and turn your workplace into a non-stop party of productivity and positivity! We want to remind you that with a sprinkle of fun, even office culture becomes a vibrant carnival of laughter and success!

Embracing Playfulness in Problem Solving: Juggling Challenges and Taming Rubber Chicken

From Puzzles to Pranks – A Playful Approach to Problem Solving

Imagine problem-solving as a maze, and you're armed with a rubber chicken instead of a map. Embrace playfulness in the face of challenges, where brainstorming sessions feel like a circus and every problem comes with its own set of clown shoes.

Juggling Challenges with a Smile: The Circus of Problem-Solving

Problem-solving is a lot like juggling flaming torches, except the torches are your everyday challenges, and instead of burning down the house, you're aiming for solutions. Master the art of juggling with a smile, where every challenge becomes an opportunity to perform your best tricks, even if those tricks involve rubber chickens.

Rubber Chickens and Innovative Solutions: The Art of Absurdity

When life hands you a rubber chicken, you don't just squawk – you innovate! Discover the magic of absurdity in problem-solving, where thinking outside the box is encouraged and creativity flows like confetti at a parade. Turn those rubber chicken moments into breakthrough solutions that leave everyone wondering, "Why didn't I think of that?"

Playful Exercises for Serious Solutions: Silly Hats and Spaghetti Structures

Get ready for a series of playful exercises that will turn your brainstorming sessions into a laugh-out-loud affair. From wearing silly hats that boost creativity to constructing structures out of spaghetti (yes, you read that right), infuse your problem-solving sessions with the kind of playfulness that leads to ingenious solutions.

Serious Fun and Playful Metrics: The Data Dance Party

Numbers and metrics might sound like a dull disco. Spice things up with a data dance party. Discover how to approach metrics with a touch of playfulness, turning data analysis into a rhythmic dance of insights. Who knew graphs and charts could groove?

Failing Forward: Bouncing Back with Bubbles and Laughter

Remember the last time you failed? Instead of sulking, imagine yourself surrounded by a cloud of bubbles, laughing your way through setbacks. Adopt a playful attitude towards failure, where each stumble is just a hilarious misstep in the dance of success. With every bounce back, you'll be armed with rubber chickens and laughter.

Creative Hurdles: From Jump Ropes to Imagination Leaps

In the world of problem-solving, hurdles are as common as coffee breaks. Turn those hurdles into jump ropes of imagination. Leap over challenges with the grace of a gazelle and the playfulness of a child on a playground.

Where Puzzles Turn into Pajama Parties and Challenges Transform into Game Shows

Imagine yourself at a puzzle-solving pajama party where challenges are as exciting as game shows. With the power of playfulness in your toolkit, you're not just solving problems – you're turning every challenge into an adventure where rubber chickens are your sidekicks and laughter is the ultimate weapon.

Remember, embracing playfulness in problem-solving isn't just about finding solutions – it's about transforming the process into a joyous journey. So, grab your rubber chicken and your thinking cap, and turn your problem-solving sessions into a circus of creativity and hilarity. With a dash of playfulness, even the most daunting challenges become opportunities to shine and laugh your way to success!

# Chapter 12

# The Humor Handbook: Crafting Playful Communication

Welcome aboard, dear entrepreneurs and business mavericks! Imagine stepping into a world where every business correspondence is less of a chore and more of a chuckle festival. Where communication isn't just about words but also about the joyous rhythm between the lines. This is the world of "Leading With Fun," and we're here to be your guides.

Elevate the Email Experience

Have you ever found yourself hovering over the 'send' button, feeling like you're dispatching another soulless piece of text into the ether? Time to jazz things up! Consider your emails as mini sketches. Could you imagine the receiver's face lighting up as they read? If not, sprinkle a dash of wit or add a quirky sign-off. Make every mail a ticket to Smileyville.

GIF it Up

In the era of digital expressions, GIFs are like the animated spice to your conversational curry. Is it a team member's birthday? Skip the drab 'happy birthday' text. Send a GIF of a dancing cat in a party hat! GIFs convey emotions, humor, and set a light-hearted tone – perfect for that dose of daily joy.

Meme-tastic Memos

Why should internet users have all the fun? The next time you want to appreciate a team member or announce a small win, do it with a meme! It's relatable, trendy, and sure to get a giggle out of everyone.

Laughter-Infused Lessons

Remember how you felt in those drawn-out training sessions? Turn the tables! Use humor to make lessons stick. Maybe a joke about how not to do things or a funny anecdote related to the topic. Laughter is not just the best medicine; it's also the best teacher.

Whistle While You Work (Or Just Laugh)

Turn routine tasks into a game. Name your projects with fun codenames. Instead of "Project X," how about "Operation Unicorn"? It's not just whimsical; it's motivational!

The Humorous Huddle

Weekly meetings can become the highlight of your team's calendar. Start with a joke of the week, use fun icebreakers, or create a humor corner where team members can share something funny. This isn't just for laughs; it sets a positive tone for the whole session.

Clever Conversations with Clients

Who said client communication has to be strictly professional? Of course, know your boundaries, but a little humor can go a long way in building rapport. A light joke or a funny analogy can make your interactions memorable.

Doodles and Drawings

Whether you're brainstorming ideas, laying out plans, or explaining concepts – make it visual. And not just any visuals, but fun doodles that convey the message. A stick figure can sometimes be more expressive than a thousand words.

Final Chuckle: Making Humor Your Communication Companion

To the esteemed leaders, creators, and dream-changers, humor is not just about cracking jokes; it's a fresh perspective, a zestier way to communicate. When you incorporate humor, you're not just speaking or writing; you're resonating. You're forming connections that go beyond business – connections built on smiles, laughter, and shared moments of joy.

So here's your call-to-action, captains of industry! Next time you draft that email, conduct that meeting, or strategize for the quarter, ask yourself: "Is there room for a chuckle?" We bet there is. Dive into the delightful world of humorous communication and watch as the magic unfolds. Lead with fun, communicate with chuckles, and transform your business into a laughter-loaded legacy!

## The Empathy Echo: Finding Humor in Human Connections

Greetings, champions of change! Dive deeper into the realm of "Leading With Fun" where connecting with the human soul isn't just an art but a playful dance. Let's infuse the very core of our business interactions with a heartfelt touch, all through the lens of humor.

### The Laughter Lens: Seeing Through Empathy

It all starts with perspective – viewing situations not just from your viewpoint but from the myriad of emotional landscapes your team and clients inhabit. When faced with a challenge or a misunderstanding, instead of reacting, ponder: "How would this look with a laughter lens?" Maybe there's a light-hearted side to it, a common ground where humor can bridge differences.

Empathetic Ears: The Power of Listening with a Smile

Often, the most genuine connections are formed when we truly listen. And sometimes, amidst the gravest of concerns, there might be room for a shared giggle. By tuning into the undertones of conversations and sensing the unspoken, you open doors for humor to waltz in.

From Puns to Pondering: Reflecting on Shared Laughs

Every humorous interaction leaves behind a footprint. It's essential to cherish and reflect on these shared laughs. They're not just moments but symbols of strengthened bonds. So, the next strategy session or team gathering you have, maybe recall that funny incident or shared joke. It's a warm reminder that amidst all the seriousness, there's always room for a hearty laugh.

The Playful Pitch: Empathetic Selling

Imagine presenting your product or idea not just as a solution but as a story interwoven with light-hearted humor. Anecdotes that tickle, analogies that amuse, and a presentation style that's brimming with empathy. Such pitches don't just sell; they connect and resonate on a human level.

### Chuckles and Challenges: Handling Objections with Humor

Let's face it; objections are part of the business. But what if, instead of getting defensive, you embrace them with a chuckle? A humorous, yet thoughtful response can defuse tension and pave the way for constructive dialogue. Remember, behind every objection is a person seeking understanding. Meet them halfway with humor.

### Leading by Laughing: Humor as a Leadership Tool

Your attitude sets the tone for your entire team. Embracing challenges with a smile, finding the silver lining in failures, and celebrating wins with shared jokes make for an inspiring leader. When you lead with laughter, you inspire resilience, creativity, and unity.

### Empathy Encore: Carrying Forward the Humorous Legacy

The journey of "Leading With Fun" is continuous. Every interaction, be it a quick chat by the water cooler or a significant business deal, is an opportunity to add a touch of humor. To truly succeed, it's essential to keep this humorous spirit alive, fostering a culture that values empathy and connection.

Dear visionaries, remember that humor is an attitude, a reflection of how we view the world and engage with it. By intertwining empathy with humor, you create an environment where people don't just work; they thrive, laugh, and grow together.

So, the next challenge you face, the next pitch you make, or the next team huddle you lead, ask yourself: "Where's the laughter in this?" Because when you find it, you find a deeper connection, a stronger bond, and a business that's not just successful but also soulful. Lead with laughter, connect with empathy, and let your business be the beacon of joy in the corporate world!

*Building Bridges with Humor: The Path to Genuine Relationships*

A hearty hello to the disruptors and dynamos! In the corporate realm, while deadlines and metrics drive us, it's the genuine human connections that sustain us. With the arsenal of humor, the journey to these profound connections becomes not only accessible but enjoyable. Delve into "Leading With Fun" and unveil the profound impact of humorous bonds.

Tales Over Tables: Dining with a Dose of Delight

When dining with clients, peers, or teams, instead of solely discussing business, weave in amusing stories from your personal life or light-hearted incidents from the office. This not only breaks the ice but also lays the foundation for genuine connections, making business discussions more fluid and less intimidating.

Feedback with Finesse: Constructive Criticism Can Be Comical

Giving feedback, especially the constructive kind, can be challenging. However, humor can be an effective buffer. For instance, "Remember when Superman wore his underwear outside? Well, this design concept reminds me of that! Let's keep the hero, but perhaps change his style?" Such analogies can soften the blow and make the feedback process interactive and engaging.

Networking Noteworthy: The Chuckles Circuit

At networking events, instead of leading with your job title, lead with a light-hearted story or a humorous observation. This approach not only makes you memorable but also makes networking less transactional and more human.

Break the Ice, But With a Joke!

Starting a new project or collaboration can be tense. Begin by sharing a funny anecdote related to the task at hand. It's a playful way to set the tone, making everyone more receptive and collaborative.

Story-Infused Sales

When reaching out to potential clients, instead of just showcasing the product, narrate a humorous story where your product played a pivotal role. It gives a human touch to the selling process, making it more relatable and memorable.

Engaging Elevator Pitches

You've got 30 seconds in an elevator with a potential investor or partner. Instead of the traditional pitch, how about a short, witty version? "Our product is like Netflix but for cat lovers. Ever thought of that?" Such pitches are not only attention-grabbing but also memorable.

Celebrations with a Twist

Marking milestones and achievements is crucial. But instead of the regular congratulatory note, how about a humorous twist? "We hit our quarterly target, so let's not dress like we're in a quarterly review tomorrow. Pajama Day, anyone?"

After Hours Amusement

After a day of brainstorming and decision-making, lighten the mood. Organize a humorous storytelling session where team members share their funniest work-related stories. It's a wonderful way to unwind and bond.

Wrap-Up Wisdom: Sustain the Spirit of Smiles

To all the innovators and initiators, remember: while tasks get completed, relationships get built. And the foundation of these relationships can be solidified with humor. It's not just about a laugh; it's about making every interaction count, making every conversation memorable, and ensuring that every collaboration is rooted in genuine understanding.

Your next endeavor awaits, trailblazers! So, as you chart new territories, remember to pack a joke, a funny story, or a witty observation. Lead with levity, connect with chuckles, and ensure your business isn't just about figures but also about fostering genuine, laughter-filled relationships.

The Ultimate Call to Action: Making Moments Matter

Esteemed pathfinders of progress, as we wind down this chapter, let us not forget the quintessential essence of our discourse. At the crossroads of humor and business lies an unprecedented realm of connection, a tapestry woven with the golden threads of laughter, smiles, and genuine moments.

Moments That Mold: Each interaction, each meeting, each correspondence is not just a transaction but an opportunity – an opportunity to touch a life, to make someone's day a tad brighter, to foster a bond that goes beyond mere business associations. Such moments are what legends are made of. And with humor, these moments become legendary.

From Laughs to Legacy: Think of the legacies that have withstood the test of time. While achievements and accolades form a part of them, it's the human touch, the stories, the moments of shared laughter that truly make them memorable. Your business has the potential to be one of these legacies. All you need is the right attitude, sprinkled with a generous dose of humor.

Carpe Diem with Chuckles: Seize the day, they say. But why just seize it when you can seize it with a chuckle? Tomorrow's success story begins with today's smile. Every task you undertake, every challenge you face, and every milestone you achieve is an opportunity to infuse joy, to create a memory, and to leave an indelible mark.

So, to all the luminaries lighting up the world of business, here's your clarion call: Embrace the power of humor. Let it be your guiding star, your secret weapon, and your trusted ally. With every email you send, every pitch you make, every product you launch, and every team you lead, weave in the magic of mirth.

Challenge yourself to lead with laughter, to forge bonds with fun, to craft connections with chuckles, and to pioneer progress with playfulness.

Remember, in the grand tapestry of business, it's not just about being the biggest or the best; it's about being the most human, the most relatable, and the most memorable. So, champions of change, set forth with fervor, armed with the most potent tool in your arsenal – humor. Go, create, lead, inspire, and most importantly, laugh. The world of "Leading With Fun" awaits you. Seize it, savor it, and make it your own!

# Chapter 13

# Leading with Fun: Harnessing Humor for Professional and Personal Success

1. The Power of Perspective: The Heartbeat of Humor

Our sense of humor is not just about the jokes we crack, the videos we share, or the laughs we have with colleagues over lunch. At its core, humor is a reflection of our "sense of perspective." It's the culmination of all the information we take in and how we choose to interpret and project it. This attitude, or our sense of humor, is a choice. Just as we decide to put on a sunny dress on a cloudy day, we decide if our humor is going to uplift or dishearten. It's time to recognize and harness the potential of this choice.

2. Communicative Comedy: The Magic of Joyful Interactions

Shift your mindset from merely being a conveyor of messages to a maestro of memorable moments. Using humor isn't about forcing a laugh but sprinkling lightness into the daily grind. Let your emails be a canvas of creativity, where wit meets information. Encourage your team to embrace emojis, craft playful signatures, and share the occasional funny anecdote. Bring levity to the boardroom because laughter is the universal language of connection.

Turn one email a day into a joy-bringer. A simple, playful sign-off or a quirky subject line can make all the difference.

3. Growing with Glee: The Sunflower Strategy

Personal development isn't just a linear journey but a dance with dips and rises. Visualize yourself not as a fixed entity but as an ever-growing sunflower, always seeking the light. This light is positivity. So, make it a habit to surround yourself with positive affirmations, constructive feedback, and environments that inspire growth. Dive deep into the treasure trove of learning, from audiobooks that enlighten to podcasts that provoke thought.

Clever Call to Action: Designate one day of the week as "Sunflower Saturday" or "Wisdom Wednesday." Dedicate this day to learning something new, whether it's a hobby, a professional skill, or a personal development podcast.

4. Building Bonds: Fertilizing Growth with Relationships

The most robust sunflowers often grow in fields, supported by the community of other blooms. Similarly, personal growth is amplified when surrounded by relationships that nurture and empower. Seek mentorship, foster deep connections, and embrace the richness of diverse perspectives. Remember, a garden of shared laughter and collective growth is the most bountiful.

Initiate a "Monthly Mentorship Meetup" at your workplace or within your community. Share stories, challenges, and celebrate successes.

5. Mindful Maintenance: Weeding Out the Negative

Growth isn't just about addition but often about subtraction. Regularly take stock of thoughts and influences that aren't serving your growth. Like a diligent gardener, prune away the negativity and make room for positive experiences and insights to flourish.

Start a "Weed-Out Wednesday." Dedicate this day to introspect, identify any negative patterns, and take steps to redirect your focus.

6. Flourishing with Flair: Celebrating Your Unique Bloom

Every sunflower is unique, and so are you. Embrace your individuality, cherish your growth journey, and remember that every day you radiate positivity is a day you make the world a little brighter.

Create a "Flourish Journal." At the end of each week, jot down three moments where you felt proud, learned something new, or brought joy to someone else.

In this ever-evolving journey of growth, always remember the power of your perspective, your unique sense of humor. Whether you're navigating the intricate corridors of corporate communications or nurturing the garden of your personal development, let your humor shine. After all, life is too short not to lead with fun.

*The Entrepreneurial Outlook: Harnessing Humor for Success*

For the high-classed entrepreneur, the vast world of business is a combination of risks, innovations, and outcomes. At the heart of this intricate dance is one's sense of perspective, or, as we'll frame it here, their sense of humor. It's more than just a laugh; it's an entrepreneur's attitude towards challenges and triumphs alike.

Strategic Laughter: Boosting Business Productivity with Humor

Every entrepreneur faces the weight of decisions, the strain of competition, and the challenges of innovation. Here, humor becomes a strategic tool. By adopting a playful perspective, entrepreneurs can foster a culture of creativity, enhancing problem-solving skills and sparking innovation. Imagine a boardroom where light-heartedness leads to the next big idea or a brainstorming session that's driven by chuckles and camaraderie.

Start your next team meeting with a light-hearted icebreaker. It might just shift the perspective enough to pave the way for fresh, innovative ideas.

Elevating Interactions: The Power of a Playful Perspective

Interactions, be they with clients, colleagues, or competitors, lay the foundation of any business venture. A humorous outlook can transform these exchanges. Instead of a mundane pitch, picture a presentation that captivates with wit and insight. Instead of a standard meeting, imagine an engaging conversation where humor builds bridges of understanding.

The Personal Touch: Infusing Humor into Branding

High-classed entrepreneurs recognize the value of branding. What if part of this branding incorporated humor? An email campaign with a touch of wit, a product launch laced with levity, or even a company slogan that brings a smile. Such branding not only stands out but also resonates, forging deeper connections with clientele.

Clever Call to Action: Re-evaluate your brand's voice. Is there room for some playful humor? A touch of wit might just be the memorable twist your brand needs.

Personal Mastery: Growing with Giggles

For the entrepreneur, personal development and business growth go hand in hand. Infusing one's journey with humor ensures a path filled with joy, resilience, and adaptability. By approaching challenges with a chuckle, embracing failures with a grin, and celebrating successes with hearty laughter, one ensures an entrepreneurial journey that's fulfilling and fruitful.

Humor in Hurdles: Embracing Setbacks with a Smile

Every entrepreneur faces setbacks. But what if, instead of sulking, one could smirk? By viewing challenges as opportunities for growth and employing humor as a coping mechanism, entrepreneurs can bounce back faster and stronger.

The next time a setback strikes, take a moment to find the humor in the situation. It might be hidden, but once uncovered, it can transform perspective and inspire renewed vigor.

To lead with fun is to embrace an attitude of positivity, resilience, and innovation. It's about recognizing the powerful choice every high-classed entrepreneur holds in framing their perspective, their humor. In the intricate dance of business and personal development, may every step be accompanied by the rhythmic beats of laughter.

## From Chuckles to Changes: Humor as a Catalyst for Innovation

In the complex ecosystem of business, it's often assumed that serious approaches yield serious results. However, a closer inspection reveals that many groundbreaking ideas stem from moments of levity. Humor, with its inherent ability to jolt us out of our usual patterns of thinking, acts as a potent catalyst for innovation.

### The Playful Mindset: Unleashing Creative Genius

The conventional and the traditional have their merits, but it's often the unconventional that brings about transformative change. A playful mindset, fueled by humor, breaks the barriers of linear thinking. It invites spontaneity, encourages risk-taking, and welcomes the unexpected. This is precisely where the magic happens. When we're playful, our minds become more fluid, allowing for connections between seemingly unrelated ideas. The result? Creative solutions that might never have been envisioned in a more rigid mindset.

Take, for instance, some of the world's most successful advertising campaigns. They weren't born from stern boardroom discussions but rather from moments of jest, playful banter, and even the occasional doodle on a napkin. It's this levity that allows for a divergence from the norm, giving birth to truly unique ideas.

Organizations Riding the Humor Wave

Modern organizations have recognized the immense potential humor holds. Companies like Google and Pixar, renowned for their innovative approaches, have seamlessly integrated fun into their workplaces. Whether it's through playful work environments, humor-infused team meetings, or creative brainstorming sessions, they've harnessed the power of laughter to foster a culture of innovation.

Google's famous 20% time policy, for example, allowed employees to spend a fifth of their working hours on personal projects that they were passionate about. While it may seem like a fun diversion, this policy birthed some of Google's most innovative products, like Gmail and AdSense.

Individual Innovators: Changing the World One Chuckle at a Time

On an individual level, countless innovators have cited humor as a driving force behind their groundbreaking ideas. The process of humor, which involves setting up an expectation and then subverting it with a punchline, mirrors the process of innovation. It's about identifying a norm (or a problem) and then overturning it with a unique solution.

Steve Jobs, a visionary in the true sense, was known for his ability to view things differently. While he took his mission seriously, he also embraced the absurdities and humor of life, using them as springboards for revolutionary ideas.

The next time you're faced with a challenge, whether in your organization or personal life, pause for a moment. Allow yourself to chuckle, to play, to diverge from the usual. Dive deep into the reservoir of humor within you. Who knows? The next big idea might just be a hearty laugh away.

As we journey through the ever-evolving landscape of business and personal growth, it's essential to remember that innovation isn't just about logic and strategy. It's about embracing the unpredictable, the humorous, the playful. Because when we lead with fun, we're not just chuckling; we're changing the world.

Unleashing the Future: A Journey Paved with Laughter

As we draw the curtains on this chapter, let's take a moment to reflect on our ultimate mission. Beyond the metrics, beyond the targets, and beyond the tangible outcomes, there lies an intangible essence - our spirit. And humor, with its vibrant colors, paints that spirit in shades of resilience, joy, and brilliance.

In the intricate ballet of business and personal evolution, humor isn't just an accompaniment; it's the rhythm that guides our movements. The chuckles that echo through boardrooms and hallways don't merely signify a fleeting moment of joy; they mark the birth of revolutionary concepts, the cementing of powerful partnerships, and the resilience to bounce back from challenges.

For every high-classed entrepreneur reading this, understand that your journey is not solely defined by the peaks you scale but by the laughter you share along the way. Each time you choose to view a setback with humor, you're not dismissing its gravity; you're merely lightening its weight on your shoulders.

Empowerment through Empathy: Recognize that every person you interact with, be it a colleague, a competitor, or a client, carries their sense of humor. It's a reflection of their life experiences, their struggles, and their triumphs. By harnessing and harmonizing these diverse senses of humor, we create symphonies of innovation and growth.

Bold Beacon for Tomorrow: Let humor be your guiding light, illuminating pathways unseen, unraveling opportunities unfathomed, and fostering connections unimagined. For when we lead with fun, we don't just enrich our present; we sculpt a future that echoes with laughter and resonates with success.

In the grand narrative of your professional and personal saga, let humor be the pen that scripts stories of victories, tales of camaraderie, and chronicles of unmatched innovation. Let's not just aim for success; let's aspire for a legacy - a legacy where every anecdote is tinted with humor, every lesson is laced with laughter, and every achievement sparkles with the iridescent glow of joy.

Forge ahead, fearless visionary, and let the world bear witness to the power of leading with fun.

# Chapter 14

# Embracing the Future: Powering Through with Purpose and Positivity

The Resonance of Resilience: A Dance of Humor and Purpose

In the vast expanse of the business realm, where challenges appear as towering mountains and competition runs fierce, a tool emerges, often underappreciated yet immensely powerful: humor. No, not the kind that solely resonates in the echoes of a hearty laugh but the deeper essence rooted in our "sense of perspective."

A Deeper Dive into Perspective

Before we jump into tales of transformation, let's unpack this profound concept. Every individual, every high-classed entrepreneur, brings to the table their unique "sense of perspective." It's akin to wearing a specific set of tinted glasses, which colors the world in a certain hue. This hue is your attitude. The way you see setbacks, the way you interpret failures, the way you celebrate victories - it all stems from this attitude.

Now, imagine if this attitude were imbued with humor. Not just the superficial kind, but the type rooted in empathy, understanding, and a zest for life. The challenges wouldn't disappear, but they'd appear less daunting. The failures would still sting, but they'd also offer lessons wrapped in chuckles. And the victories? They'd sound like triumphant symphonies laced with laughter.

Stories of Unyielding Spirits

Across the boardrooms of Silicon Valley to the startups of Silicon Alley, tales abound of leaders who've turned the tide, not by sheer grit alone but by coupling it with humor. They've faced downturns, rejections, and even crises. Yet, their attitude, their humor-infused perspective, turned these adversities into stepping stones.

Take, for instance, a CEO of a budding tech firm who, upon facing a significant product failure, gathered his team and instead of a stern reprimand, started the meeting with a comical anecdote related to the mishap. The room, initially tense, soon filled with laughter. This shift in mood didn't downplay the gravity of the failure but reframed it. The team, rejuvenated and relaxed, approached the problem with fresh eyes, leading to quicker and more innovative solutions.

Or consider a high-classed entrepreneur who, after a pitch rejection, didn't dwell on the disappointment. Instead, she chose to humorously narrate the experience in her vlog, extracting the lessons while lightening the mood. Her followers not only connected with her vulnerability but were inspired by her humor-driven resilience. The episode became a testament to turning setbacks into comebacks.

Your Journey, Your Choice

Every high-classed entrepreneur, every visionary stands at a crossroads. On one side lies the path of rigidity, and on the other, a journey sprinkled with humor. The challenges remain consistent, but the journey's flavor changes dramatically based on the chosen path.

So, the next time adversity knocks on your door, welcome it with a smile, maybe even a chuckle. Dive deep into your reservoir of humor, draw from your unique sense of perspective, and transform challenges into opportunities. After all, resilience isn't just about bouncing back; it's about bouncing back with a laugh, ready to face another day in the thrilling saga of entrepreneurship.

Purposeful Positivity: Lighting Up Organizations One Laugh at a Time

In the vast, intricate landscape of the corporate world, a beacon shines, often overlooked yet astoundingly powerful: a positive mindset. While many associate this mindset with individual growth, its potential to reshape entire organizations remains largely untapped. Now, let's sprinkle this positivity with the magic dust of humor, and we have a formula potent enough to revolutionize workplaces.

The Deep-Rooted Impact of an Uplifted Perspective

Every single interaction, decision, and strategy in a corporate setting is influenced by the collective attitude of its members. And at the heart of this attitude lies our "sense of perspective." When humor, derived from our unique viewpoint, is woven into the fabric of daily operations, the results are nothing short of transformative.

Imagine a team brainstorming session where every idea is welcomed with an open heart, a chuckle, and an enthusiastic 'What if?'. Instead of the fear of judgment, there's the thrill of exploration. Instead of rigid hierarchies, there's a fluid exchange of creativity. This is the power of positivity, amplified by humor.

Rippling Effects of Radiant Resonance

A single droplet of positivity, charged with humor, creates ripples that spread across the vast ocean of organizational operations. These aren't mere waves; they're transformative currents.

- Team Morale: A team that laughs together bonds together. Positive humor eases tensions, breaks barriers, and fosters camaraderie. This isn't about merely keeping spirits high; it's about building a resilient foundation that thrives on collective joy.
- Operational Brilliance: When challenges are approached with a light-hearted perspective, problem-solving becomes a delightful puzzle rather than a daunting task. The blend of humor and positivity promotes out-of-the-box thinking, ensuring solutions that are not just effective but also innovative.
- Visionary Triumphs: Long-term visions are no longer mere targets to achieve but exciting adventures to embark upon. An organization steeped in positivity and humor envisions a future where success is measured not just in numbers but in the joy of the journey.

Leading with Levity

For the high-classed entrepreneur, humor becomes more than just an occasional relief; it's a strategic tool. By fostering a culture where humor-driven positivity is the norm, they set the stage for unparalleled growth. Not just of profits and portfolios, but of people, partnerships, and possibilities.

So, the next time you find yourself amidst the hustle and bustle of your organizational duties, take a moment to reflect. How can you infuse today's tasks with a dose of humor? How can you light up your team's spirit with a touch of positivity? Remember, every chuckle shared, every positive affirmation exchanged, and every humorous insight embraced paves the way for a brighter, more successful tomorrow.

Think of that one change, that one humorous spin you can introduce to your daily operations. Embrace it, implement it, and watch the wonders of purposeful positivity unfold. Because in the grand tapestry of organizational success, humor and positivity aren't mere threads; they're the vibrant colors that make the masterpiece come alive.

## Visionaries with Vigor: Leaders Who Laugh and Lead

The corporate world often paints a picture of stern-faced leaders pacing boardrooms with intensity. But scratch beneath the surface, and you'll find visionaries who've tapped into the transformative power of humor, using it not just as a stress-reliever but as a leadership tool. These are leaders who've understood that our "sense of perspective," or our humor, is more than just a laugh; it's a reflection of our attitude. And they've chosen an attitude that uplifts, connects, and innovates.

Redefining the Boardroom Beat

1. The Inclusive Innovator

One CEO of a burgeoning tech startup made it a ritual to begin board meetings with a humorous anecdote or a playful icebreaker. This wasn't just for laughs. It set the tone for an inclusive environment where every voice, no matter how unconventional, was valued. This sense of inclusion led to a workspace where creativity wasn't just encouraged; it was celebrated. The company's products? Just as imaginative as their brainstorming sessions, capturing markets and hearts alike.

Empathy Insight: Put yourself in the shoes of an employee. How would it feel to be in a room that buzzes with creativity and chuckles? It's an environment where risks are taken, mistakes are learned from, and innovation flourishes.

2. The Compassionate Captain

A renowned leader in the healthcare sector was known for her unique feedback sessions. Instead of mundane performance reviews, she'd engage team members in humorous role-reversals, often playing the role of a mischievous intern. This approach, rooted deeply in her "sense of perspective," transformed feedback from a dreaded chore to a much-anticipated event. The outcome? Enhanced employee satisfaction, lower attrition rates, and a team that looked forward to growth and feedback.

Empathy Insight: Imagine the relief and genuine connection that comes from such a refreshing approach to feedback. It's not just about growth; it's about growing together with a smile.

3. The Disruptive Dreamer

Leading a cutting-edge design agency, this entrepreneur made headlines for his "Fun Fridays," where the entire day was dedicated to exploring playful designs, humorous concepts, and even the occasional office prank. While competitors raised eyebrows, clients were enamored. This humor-centric approach wasn't just fun; it was disruptive. It churned out designs that stood out, campaigns that resonated, and a brand that was synonymous with creativity.

Empathy Insight: In a world drowning in content and design, imagine the magnetism of something that makes you smile. It's not just about being seen; it's about being remembered.

Anchoring Aspirations with Action: Making Dreams Dance with Daily Deeds

Dreams and visions form the bedrock of any successful journey. Yet, it's the daily dance of actions, often infused with that delightful sense of perspective - our humor - that truly transforms these lofty aspirations into tangible triumphs. In the world of business and self-development, it's not just about aiming for the stars; it's about lighting the way with every step, every chuckle, and every innovative idea.

1. The Daily Dose of Delight

Every morning, as the day unfurls its potential, make it a ritual to start with a moment of humor. It could be a light joke, a funny video clip, or even a humorous quote. This isn't mere frivolity. It sets the tone for the day, reminding us of our innate ability to perceive things through an uplifting lens, thus shaping our attitude.

Empathy Insight: Envision the ripple effects of starting your day with a smile. Challenges seem surmountable, interactions more engaging, and solutions appear within grasp.

2. Meetings with Mirth

Transform mundane meetings into brainstorming sessions where humor acts as a catalyst for creativity. Let the agenda include a few minutes for sharing a humorous incident or a light-hearted anecdote. This not only breaks the ice but also fosters an environment of trust and open communication. It's in these moments that the seeds of innovation are often sown.

Empathy Insight: Think about the camaraderie that humor can cultivate. In an atmosphere of laughter, barriers break down, hierarchies dissolve, and true collaboration takes root.

3. Task-lists Tinged with Playfulness

While charting out daily tasks, add a playful twist. Name tasks creatively, infuse breaks with short, fun activities, or even gamify mundane chores. As you approach work with this rejuvenated sense of perspective, you'll find productivity soaring, not because of the pressure, but because of the sheer joy of accomplishment.

Empathy Insight: Visualize a workday where tasks aren't burdens but challenges approached with enthusiasm. When tasks transform into playful puzzles, the journey becomes as rewarding as the destination.

4. Feedback with Finesse and Fun

Feedback, often a daunting word, can be reimagined through the lens of humor. While providing constructive criticism, lace it with encouraging humor. Highlight mistakes with playful metaphors, ensuring the focus remains on growth and learning. This approach not only softens the blow but also makes the feedback actionable and acceptable.

Empathy Insight: Put yourself in the shoes of a team member receiving feedback. The difference between a drab critique and one laced with humor is the difference between defensiveness and eagerness to improve.

The Actionable Nudge: Today, as you chart your course towards your grand vision, remember the power your sense of perspective holds. Let every action, no matter how small, be a reflection of this vibrant attitude. Choose humor that encourages, uplifts, and drives forward. Remember, in the intricate tapestry of success, every thread of humor weaves patterns of unparalleled brilliance. Embrace this, and let every giggle guide you, every chuckle chart your course, and every smile signal success on the horizon.

The Transformative Power of Perspective: A Tapestry of Triumphs, Trials, and Tickles

Perspective, the lens through which we view the world, dictates not just our responses but also shapes the narrative of our journey. When this sense of perspective melds seamlessly with humor, it creates a potent amalgamation that equips high-classed entrepreneurs with the ability to view every situation as a canvas – sometimes painted with lessons, sometimes with opportunities, and at other times with moments of sheer jubilation.

1. Perception and Prowess

Our sense of perspective, rooted deeply in our personal experiences, beliefs, and attitudes, acts as a compass guiding our interactions, decisions, and reactions. For the high-classed entrepreneur, integrating humor into this perspective offers a distinct advantage. It becomes less about navigating challenges and more about embracing them with a mindset primed for growth and innovation.

Empathy Insight: Imagine facing a setback. The weight feels significantly lighter when approached with a touch of humor, turning a stumbling block into a stepping stone.

2. From Challenges to Chortles

Every entrepreneurial journey is paved with uncertainties and unforeseen challenges. Yet, when humor, defined as our unique sense of perspective, intertwines with these challenges, they transform. What might initially appear as obstacles metamorphose into opportunities for learning, growth, and sometimes, an unexpected chuckle.

Empathy Insight: Visualize a misstep or a failed venture. Now, reimagine it with a sprinkle of humor. The scenario shifts from a mood of despondency to one of reflection, resilience, and renewed vigor.

3. Opportunities Amplified with Optimism

Our perspective, when soaked in the hues of humor, amplifies opportunities. Deals, partnerships, or innovations are approached not just with seriousness but with a zest and zeal that often paves the way for out-of-the-box thinking and solutions that resonate on a deeper, more human level.

Empathy Insight: Think of a high-stakes business meeting. The ambiance changes dramatically when there's room for a genuine smile or a light-hearted moment, leading to connections that are not just professional but profoundly personal.

4. Celebrations Beyond Success Metrics

True, numbers matter. But for the high-classed entrepreneur who intertwines their sense of perspective with humor, celebrations go beyond balance sheets and profit margins. Every little achievement, be it a successful pitch, a product launch, or even a day without hiccups, becomes a cause for celebration.

Empathy Insight: Recall a personal achievement, no matter how minor it might seem. When viewed through the humor-tinted glasses of perspective, it becomes a moment of pure joy, a testament to one's journey, and a promise of the path ahead.

The Nudge to Action: Today, as you stride forward in your entrepreneurial journey, take a moment to assess your perspective. Are you allowing enough room for humor? Remember, each chuckle, each light-hearted moment, isn't a deviation from the path but rather an affirmation of it. As you harness the transformative power of perspective, ensure that it's painted in vibrant shades of humor. For in this unique blend lies the secret to not just achieving success but truly relishing the journey towards it.

Motivational Momentum: Propelled by Perspective and Positivity

Momentum, in the world of physics, is defined as the quantity of motion an object possesses. In the realm of high-classed entrepreneurship, it represents the wave of progress, the drive that pushes one forward, and the force that ensures consistent growth. Yet, maintaining this momentum is a challenge that even the most seasoned professionals grapple with. However, by integrating a unique sense of humor – our personalized attitude – into the dynamics of momentum, the journey becomes not just sustainable but also joyfully exhilarating.

1. The Dynamics of Driven Development

Every entrepreneur experiences those golden moments of progress, where everything seems to align perfectly. However, the real magic lies in harnessing this energy and ensuring it doesn't dissipate. By viewing challenges and triumphs through the humorous lens of perspective, entrepreneurs can create a resilient buffer against setbacks, ensuring that momentum remains unbroken.

Empathy Insight: Remember a time when things went astray? Now, infuse that memory with a touch of humor. Suddenly, it's not a wall blocking progress but a mere bump in the road, easily navigable.

2. Fueling Forward Motion with Fun

While determination and grit are crucial components in maintaining momentum, humor adds the spark that makes the journey worthwhile. Using wit, levity, and a positive attitude, entrepreneurs can turn daily routines into a series of delightful experiences, ensuring that the journey forward is both productive and pleasurable.

Empathy Insight: Envision a long workday. Now, sprinkle in moments of laughter, witty exchanges, and light-hearted banter. The day transforms from a mundane task-list to a series of memorable moments, each propelling you further on your path.

3. Personal and Professional Evolution: A Journey Marked by Mirth

As entrepreneurs evolve, so do their goals, aspirations, and challenges. By intertwining personal and professional development with humor, the process of growth becomes a delightful dance, where every step, twist, and turn is marked by a chuckle or a reflective smile.

Empathy Insight: Think of a personal goal you've recently achieved. Now, reminisce about the journey with all its ups and downs but viewed through a humor-tinted perspective. The entire narrative shifts, with moments of stress transforming into learning episodes, each punctuated by a dose of humor.

4. The Boundary-Pushing Power of Positivity

When momentum is paired with a humor-laden perspective, boundaries blur, and horizons expand. What might seem like unattainable targets become achievable milestones. By adopting a humor-infused attitude, entrepreneurs find themselves constantly pushing the envelope, exploring uncharted territories, and setting benchmarks that are not just about numbers but also about the quality of the journey.

Empathy Insight: Visualize a challenging target. Now, imagine approaching it with a humor-filled strategy. The challenge becomes an exciting quest, each obstacle a humorous anecdote waiting to be told.

The Nudge to Action: Today, as you find yourself riding the wave of momentum, take a moment to check the fuel powering your journey. Is it just determination? Or is it enriched with the vibrant energy of humor? Remember, in the grand odyssey of entrepreneurship, it's not just about moving forward; it's about savoring every moment of the journey. So, as you set your sights on the horizon, ensure your sails are billowed with gusts of laughter and perspective. For in this harmonious blend lies the secret to not just sustaining momentum but truly reveling in it.

## The Legacy of Leading with Laughter: Visionaries in a World Afloat with Joy

In the annals of business history, numerous metrics gauge success. Profits, market shares, and innovation indices have traditionally crowned the victors. Yet, as we stand at this junction, envision a future where success isn't just measured by graphs, percentages, or financial reports. Imagine a world where enterprises are celebrated for the smiles they invoke, the chuckles they inspire, and the heartwarming laughter they spread across boardrooms and beyond. This is not just a whimsical dream but a compelling vision of what can be.

### 1. The Currency of Contentment

While financial stability is paramount, there's an intangible wealth waiting to be tapped – the wealth of joy. By interlacing business objectives with humor, organizations won't just meet their targets; they'll redefine them. The success stories of tomorrow won't be just about soaring stock prices but also about the radiant waves of positive energy that ripple through every stakeholder connected to the enterprise.

Empathy Insight: Reflect on your most rewarding business moments. Beyond the deal closures and accolades, didn't the shared laughter and camaraderie make those victories even more memorable?

2. Pioneering Positive Impacts

Using humor as a guiding philosophy, businesses can create profound positive impacts. From fostering nurturing work cultures that prioritize mental well-being to forging client relationships that go beyond transactions, every interaction becomes an opportunity to spread joy.

Empathy Insight: Remember a business meeting where genuine laughter eased tensions and led to breakthrough solutions. Now, visualize such interactions as the norm rather than the exception.

3. Sculpting Legacies Etched in Elation

While material achievements are commendable, it's the legacies of love, positivity, and joy that endure. By embracing the humor-filled perspective as defined by our senses, businesses can transition from mere corporate entities to beacons of positivity, leaving indelible marks not just on industries but on hearts.

Empathy Insight: Envision a world where company anniversaries celebrate not just years of operation but moments of shared joy, humor-inspired innovations, and the countless smiles spread both within and outside their walls.

A Charge to Champion: As we gaze ahead, let's not be mere spectators of this vibrant world. Let's be the trailblazers. For every entrepreneur and leader reading this, realize that you hold the paintbrush. You can color the canvas of your professional journey and the broader business landscape with strokes of humor, empathy, and joy.

Let the essence of this book, the spirit of "Leading With Fun : Infusing Joy and Laughter into Every Day," not just be words on a page but a clarion call. A call to infuse humor into every strategy, every interaction, and every decision. Let's not wait for this joy-filled future; let's sculpt it, one chuckle at a time. Embrace the attitude, the perspective, and lead your teams, businesses, and communities into an era where laughter is not just the best medicine but the very soul of success.

www.ingramcontent.com/pod-product-compliance
Lightning Source LLC
LaVergne TN
LVHW030311070526
838199LV00008B/373